D1569635

COMMODITY SPREADS

COMMODITY SPREADS

ANALYSIS, SELECTION, AND TRADING TECHNIQUES

By

COURTNEY SMITH

TRADERS PRESS, INC.
P.O. Box 10344
Greenville, S.C. 29603

*Books for Stock
and Commodity
Traders*

ISBN: 0-934380-15-5

Publications of TRADERS PRESS, INC.:

Commodity Spreads: A Historical Chart Perspective (Dobson)
Commodity Spreads: Volume 2 (Dobson)
The Trading Rule That Can Make You Rich* (Dobson)
Viewpoints of a Commodity Trader (Longstreet)
Commodities: A Chart Anthology (Dobson)
Profitable Grain Trading (Ainsworth)
A Complete Guide to Trading Profits (Paris)
Trader's Guide to Technical Analysis (Hardy)
The Professional Commodity Trader (Kroll)
Jesse Livermore: Speculator-King (Sarnoff)
Reminiscences of a Stock Operator (Lefevre)
Understanding Fibonacci Numbers (Dobson)
**Wall Street Ventures & Adventures through
     Forty Years** (Wyckoff)
Winning Market Systems (Appel)
Commodity Spreads (Smith)

Reprinted by agreement with the author, Courtney Smith

Published November 1988

TRADERS PRESS, INC.
P.O. Box 10344
Greenville, S.C. 29603

*Books for Stock
and Commodity
Traders*

COMMODITY SPREADS: ANALYSIS, SELECTION, AND TRADING TECHNIQUES

INTRODUCTION

The study of commodity spreads is a subject with which I am well familiar, having spent three years of weekends in libraries in the early 1970's doing the research and charting (by hand!) that culminated in the 1975 publication of my own first book, COMMODITY SPREADS: A HISTORICAL CHART PERSPECTIVE. This fascinating topic has always been of special interest to me; however, the reference material on it has always been sparse. I was delighted in 1982 when this book was first published (by my friend and former colleague at Paine Webber, Courtney Smith) as it provided a long needed and well done guide to the analysis and trading of spreads. I was equally disappointed when the book (previously published under a different title) went out of print. Constantly asked by TRADERS PRESS customers for a good book on spread analysis, I soon tired of telling them that none were available because the best one I knew of had gone out of print. In keeping with the TRADERS PRESS philosophy of meeting the educational needs of the commodity trader, I decided to do all possible to bring back into print this excellent book. Let me express to author Courtney Smith, on my own behalf and for all spread traders, a profound THANKS for the right to publish this 1988 TRADERS PRESS reprint of his book.

TRADERS PRESS specializes in the publication and distribution of books of interest to stock, option, and commodity traders. Our catalog lists and describes nearly two hundred books dealing with technical analysis, trading systems, methods and technqiues, and other topics of interest to the trader. To receive a free copy of our current catalog, write us at P.O. Box 10344, Greenville, S.C. 29603.

Greenville, S.C.
October, 1988

EDWARD D. DOBSON, President
TRADERS PRESS, INC.

Books for Stock and Commodity Traders
Serving traders since 1975

Preface

Spread trading is an integral part of the commodity futures market-place, yet relatively little has been written about spreads. There are more fingers on one hand than books about spreads.

Most books present little more than a cursory look at spread analysis. Fortunately, there are several good reference texts on historical spread price action. This book concentrates on the analysis of spreads and spread price action. Spread analysis is aimed at the discovery and execution of profitable spread trades. The historical spread texts are simply one of the tools the spread analyst uses.

Commodity periodicals have provided most of the published material about spreads. The articles in these periodicals make up the bulk of commodity spread literature. Their value ranges from useless to exciting. The trader often wonders about the utility of a ten-year-old article.

A number of advisory newsletters dedicated to spreads have come and most have gone. They generally offer rationales for their spread recommendations, which help by providing the reader with a look over the analyst's shoulder, to discover what factors are important. Newsletters dedicated to spread trading have been written as often from a fundamental as from a technical viewpoint. In other words, the analyst was looking at supply and demand information as much as at price action. This is quite different from the commodity advisory letters that recommend outright purchases and sales. Most of these concentrate on price action and only incidentally look at the fundamentals.

A few traders have been fortunate enough to have known an experienced spread trader well enough to have been able to learn from him. This allows the student to interact with the teacher. The novice can ask questions of the more experienced trader and get immediate answers.

Over the years, there have been spread seminars, often sponsored by commodity brokerage firms. The seminars have been of an introductory nature and have provided little information on spread analysis. However, they have provided the opportunity for inquisitive attendees to ask questions of the experts giving the seminars.

This book contains basic spread analysis techniques which, I hope, will stimulate readers to do their own research. Along with the lack of literature on spreads, there has been a lack of spread analysts. A goal of this book is to increase interest in spreads and provide the marketplace of ideas with a larger supply of spread trading analysts.

The techniques in this book will not make you a millionaire overnight. They certainly haven't made me one. On the other hand, they have provided significant profits when most traders were taking losses. Each reader of this book will acquire something different from it. Some traders will be attracted to the technical analysis, while others will prefer the fundamental and statistical analysis.

The key to the successful use of this book lies in trying the methods outlined. Only through experience can traders understand what is being said. After reading this book, traders still must find the method they feel is the most profitable and best fits their perspective on the market, the one they feel most comfortable with.

Courtney Smith

Chicago, Illinois
August 1982

Acknowledgments

A number of people have contributed ideas, criticism, and help to the writing of this book. Their input is greatly appreciated.

Jack Grushcow provided inspiration and encouragement and taught me much of what is in this book. I would like to thank Paul Burns for his superlative and insightful job of editing and for his many worthwhile suggestions. I am grateful to the Literary Executor of the late Sir Ronald A. Fisher, F.R.S., to Dr. Frank Yates, F.R.S., and to Longman Group Ltd., London, for permission to reprint tables from their book *Statistical Tables for Biological, Agricultural and Medical Research* (6th Edition, 1974). In preparing the manuscript, Janet Maas took on a hard job and did it well. Lee Turnbull contributed ideas and encouragement when they were hard to come by. Jim McKeever helped me get started in the right direction with the right concepts. The patience of my editor, Stephen Kippur, is greatly appreciated.

To Tari Gallagher, thank you.

C. S.

Contents

ONE

Introduction

Over the years, commodity markets have increasingly caught the attention of investors and the general public. The rapidly escalating prices of 1973 probably did more to spark this interest than any event in recent times. Increasing volume and increasing value have been the hallmarks of commodity markets for many years.

In spite of the greater interest in commodities, spread trading has received little attention. Spread trading is the simultaneous purchase of one commodity futures contract and sale of a different contract. The contracts can be different delivery months in the same commodity; they can be two different commodities that are related; they can be the same commodity traded in two different locations.

Spread trading has always been an important part of the commodity futures marketplace. Large commercial firms are often large spreaders and analyze and utilize commodity spreads in many ways. As a simple example, commercial firms frequently use spreads to move their hedges from one contract month to another. They trade spreads in an effort to recover the costs of storing and financing their inventories. They examine spreads to determine where they will deliver their particular commodity. These are but a few of the ways in which commercial firms utilize commodity spreads.

Large speculators are also heavy users of commodity spreads. It is not uncommon for large speculators to have more than one-third of their positions in spreads. Let's look at the wheat market as an example. On November 30, 1980, large speculative traders had 80% of their

1

contracts involved in spreads! Why large speculators are so interested in spreads is examined in Chapter 3.

Nearly all spread trades are traded by either the large speculators or the commercial firms. These sophisticated participants in the commodity futures market are knowledgeable about spreads and extensive users of spread trading techniques. On the other hand, the small speculator is an infrequent user of spreads.

There are a number of possible reasons why small speculators don't trade spreads frequently. It could be that small speculators don't trade spreads because of the greater complexity of analysis: they must analyze two positions instead of one. The fundamentalist will have to analyze the relative supply and demand of two contracts rather than just the overall supply and demand. Analysis of relative supply and demand is a very subtle problem. It could also be that the majority of small speculators are not familiar enough with fundamentals to trade spreads. Most analysis of spreads centers around fundamental analysis, where most speculative analysis of outright positions centers around technical analysis.

In spite of this, the small speculator should be vitally interested in spreads. For reasons that are explained more fully in Chapter 3, the small speculator can improve profit potential by trading spreads properly. As the prices and volatility of commodity futures contracts increase, there becomes an even greater need for information on spread trading. Spread trading can provide a vehicle to decrease the volatility and the risk of futures trading. The two major approaches to analyzing commodity futures are called fundamental analysis and technical analysis.

Fundamental analysis is directed primarily toward the elucidation and analysis of the supply and demand situation. The fundamentalist will look at such factors as planting, exports, crop production, domestic disappearance, weather, and currency fluctuations. Fundamental analysis seeks not only to discover the factors that go into making the current price what it is but also to predict what those factors will be in the future.

Technical analysis can consider only those factors the marketplace itself is composed of. The technician will look at such things as price action, volume, and open interest to help determine an opinion of the market. The technician largely seeks to either describe or predict the market action. That is, she or he tries to describe the present market action and assumes that the current situation will continue in the future. The descriptive technician assumes that a market will continue for a long enough time to create a profitable trade. The predictive technician tries to discover technical factors which give insight into the future of prices and is less concerned with the marketplace as it exists.

Many people believe the fundamentalist has the harder task. The sources of information, the sheer weight of the information, and the greater depth of insight necessary to analyze the information are all factors that make the fundamentalist's job more difficult.

It is no accident that the state of the art of technical analysis is more advanced than that of fundamental analysis. There are many books written about how to analyze the market using a technical basis. Books detailing fundamental analysis, however, are rare.

Both types of analysis are discussed in every chapter of this book, except Chapter 11, which is devoted entirely to some of the classic ideas of technical analysis.

The book is organized with the basics of spread trading in the first several chapters and the more esoteric subjects in the late chapters.

Chapter 2 answers the question "What is a spread?" and is directed at either the novice or the experienced trader who wants a review. It is recommended that all readers look at this chapter. Many terms in spread trading are confusing or contradictory. For example, the term "spread" can refer to both the subject of this book or the distance between the bid and ask prices for a commodity. Chapter 2 defines the conventions that are followed in the remainder of the book.

Chapter 3 outlines some of the reasons why a trader should trade spreads. It also looks at some of the reasons why a trader who doesn't want to trade spreads should still follow spread price action. Answers are given from the point of view of large speculators, small speculators, and hedgers.

Chapter 4 is a discussion of some of the reasons that spread prices move. We look briefly at the random walk theory as well as arguments against it. We look at some of the interaction of the participants in the marketplace that suggest why spreads move. This chapter, though speculative, provides the rationale and framework for much of the analysis that follows.

Chapter 5 is a detailed analysis of carrying charges. The chapter examines how to calculate them and what can make them change in value.

Chapter 6 is an extension of the concepts outlined in Chapter 5. Techniques are given for trading spreads that are close to the full cost of storage, insurance, and financing. The chapter also discusses how to profit from changes in the carrying charges.

Chapter 7 is devoted to the techniques involved in bull and bear spreading. Bull and bear spreads are often used as substitutes for outright positions. Techniques for this purpose as well as techniques of analysis are considered here.

Chapter 8 is the first of two chapters that use historical information in analyzing commodity spreads. The techniques center around discovering years that have similar fundamentals and then analyzing the predicted price behavior on that basis.

Chapter 9 discusses historical comparisons of previous price behaviors rather than previous fundamental factors. There is a discussion of the various methods of determining seasonal price behavior.

Chapter 10 presents probably the first published discussion of linear regression and correlation analysis of commodity spreads. These forms of analysis attempt to quantify the effects of changes in the supply and demand factors on the price of the spread. Although this chapter has a great amount of mathematics, the math looks harder than it is.

Chapter 11 outlines some of the classic approaches to the broad area called technical analysis. This is a discussion of chart patterns in relation to spreads.

Chapter 12 looks at those things that are unique to intermarket spreads. Several of the more important spreads of this type are examined.

Chapter 13 looks at spreads between different commodities and the factors that are unique to the trading of them.

Chapter 14 outlines the construction of a trading plan. A sample trading plan and a method of weekly updating are presented.

Chapter 15 is a potpourri of trading tips that don't fit into any other chapter, and Chapter 16 lists sources of further information.

In summary, the book provides an introduction to the basic concepts of spread trading as well as an outline of more advanced techniques.

TWO

Spreads and Spread Terminology

Before we go any further let us clear up some of the confusion surrounding the nomenclature of spreads. The word "spread" itself is not universally accepted. In New York, "straddle" and "switch" are often used. In this book, we use the term "spread"—but remember, this is not the only term.

A *spread* is the purchase of one futures contract and the simultaneous sale of another futures contract. The spread trader becomes simultaneously long one futures contract and short another futures contract.

A spread is composed of two *legs*. The *long contract* is one leg and the *short contract* is the other leg.

Spreads can be between time and/or location and/or commodity. An example of a spread between time would be September lumber versus November lumber. One can also spread different commodities, such as wheat and corn. One can even spread different markets such as Kansas City wheat and Chicago wheat. Another example of a location spread is London silver versus New York silver.

A spread which is between different contract months in the same commodity is called an *interdelivery* or *intercommodity spread*, while a spread between different commodities is called an *intercommodity spread*. The examples of spreading commodities in different markets are *intermarket spreads*.

5

When one trades spreads, one is trying to profit on the change in the difference in price between the two contracts. The spread trader is concerned with the relative prices of two contracts rather than the absolute level of prices. This is not to say that the price level of a commodity does not affect the spread, but this is not the way the spread trader makes money. Let's look at an example of an intracommodity spread.

Let's say that on May 1, 1976, you had sold one December 1976 contract of copper at 73¢ and simultaneously bought one May 1977 contract of copper at 74¢. The difference in price was 1¢ in favor of the May contract. Your margin would have been about $250. On August 6, 1976, the difference between December and May copper has widened to 3¢. (The December contract was selling for 70¢ and the May, for 73¢.) Because of carrying charges (which are explained later) you knew that the spread was not likely to widen any further. You liquidated the position by buying the December contract and selling the May contract. Your profit comes to $500 minus roughly $60 commission for a net profit of $440. Nearly 200% on your money in three months! Let me put this transaction in chart form:

Date	Action Taken
May 1, 1976	Sell one contract December 1976 copper at 73¢ per pound.
	Buy one contract May 1977 copper at 74¢ per pound.
Aug 6, 1976	Buy one contract December 1976 copper at 70¢ per pound.
	Sell one contract May 1977 copper at 73¢ per pound.

The result is:

3¢ per pound gain on December 1976 contract × 25,000 pounds.
1¢ per pound loss on May 1977 contract × 25,000 pounds.

$750 gain on December 1976 minus $30 commission equals $720 net profit.

$250 loss on May 1977 contract plus $30 commission equals $280 net loss.

$720 profit on December 1976 contract minus $280 loss on May 1977 contract equals $440 net profit on spread.

Interdelivery spreads are subdivided into two types, the bull spread and the bear spread. We discuss the bull and bear spreads in much greater detail in Chapter 7, where you will see some exceptions to the rules mentioned below.

The trader is long the nearby contract and short the deferred contract in a *bull spread*. An example of a bull spread is long May 1978 copper and short December 1978 copper. The trader who has a bull spread is looking for the nearby contract to be stronger than the deferred contract. In other words, if the absolute price levels are rising, the trader is looking for the nearby to rise more than the deferred. Conversely, if the absolute price level is declining, the trader is looking for the nearby contract to decline less than the deferred. Of course, there is always the possibility the nearby will gain in price and the deferred will decline in price.

The *bear spread* is the reverse of the bull spread. The trader is short the nearby month and long the deferred month and is therefore looking for the deferred month to be relatively stronger than the nearby month. An example of a bear spread is short October 1982 hogs and long February 1983 hogs.

INTERCROP SPREADS

Another type of intracommodity spread is the intercrop spread. This entails taking a long position in one crop year and a short position in a different crop year. For example, the crop year for Kansas City wheat begins with the July contract and ends with the following May contract. A trader who is long the May 1981 contract and short the July 1981 contract would be in an intercrop spread. Note, however, that being long the July 1981 contract and short the May 1982 contract is not an intercrop spread, because those particular two months are in the same crop year.

There is a significantly greater amount of volatility in intercrop spreads than in the nonintercrop interdelivery spreads. As a result, margins are often higher. A dramatic example of an intercrop spread is the August pork bellies versus the February contract of the following calendar year. The crop year in pork bellies, for futures market purposes, is from February to August. The exchange rules dictate that August pork bellies may not be redelivered against the following

February pork bellies. So, although the two contracts are in the same commodity, they are governed by different supply and demand considerations. It is therefore quite possible for August and February bellies to move in opposite directions. Although there is significantly more volatility, there is also greater profit potential.

Table 2.1 is a list of the various commodities and their crop years in futures markets contracts. The price of an intracommodity spread is

Table 2.1 Commodity Crop Years

	Crop Year	
Commodity	First Future	Last Future
Wheat		
K.C., Chi.	July	May
Minneapolis	September	July
Corn	December	September
Oats	July	May
Soybeans	September	August
Soybean oil	October	September
Soybean meal	October	September
Live hogs	None	None
Frozen pork bellies	February	August
Cattle—live	None	None
Cattle—feeder	None	None
Treasury bonds	None	None
Treasury bills	None	None
GNMA	None	None
Lumber	None	None
Plywood	None	None
Foreign currencies	None	None
Cotton	October	July
Frozen concentrated orange juice	January	November
Potatoes	November	April
Cocoa	December	September
Coffee	December	September
Sugar	None	None
Platinum	None	None
Heating oil	None	None

5¢ = $250

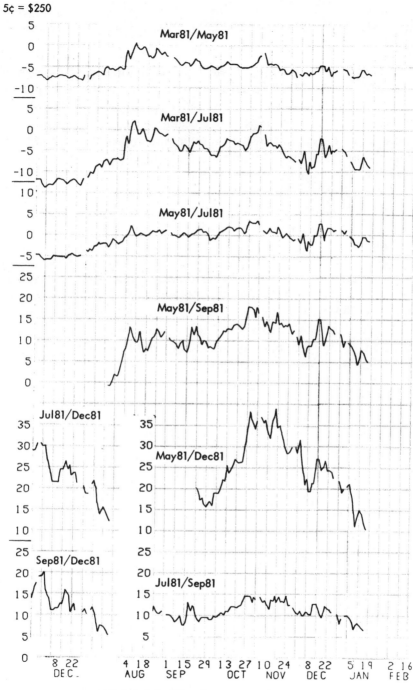

Figure 2.1   March/July corn spread.

9

the difference between the two contracts. A trader who was long December corn at $3.00 and short March corn at $3.10 was bull spread December/March corn at 10¢ premium the March. An alternative way to say this is to say the trader was in the spread at March 10¢ over December. Note that if December rises above March, we would quote the spread at, for example, December 12¢ over March. Thus one has to specify the differences in value between the contracts as well as which contract is the premium month.

Figure 2.1 shows the price behavior of the March 1981/July 1981 corn spread. The price started at around 12¢ premium the July and moved up to a high of around 2¢ premium the March where it began a choppy downtrend until, at the end of the chart, it traded at about 9¢ premium the July. (The prices on this spread chart, as well as all other spread charts in this book, are the differences between settlement prices.) The trader should note that the contract differences are plotted in cents per bushel. As we will see later, other types of spreads are graphed as the difference in dollar value between the two spread contracts. All intracommodity spreads are graphed and quoted as the unit difference between the contracts.

Spreads are always quoted with the long contract given first. Thus the trader would initiate a long July wheat/short May wheat trade but would not initiate a short May wheat/long July wheat trade. Even though the short contract may be chronologically first, the long contract is always the first quoted.

INTERCOMMODITY SPREADS

An intercommodity spread is a spread between two different commodities. An example is long December gold and short December silver. Although it is not necessary in an intercommodity spread to spread the same months in the two different commodities, it is the more common action. Intercommodity spreads should be thought of as spreads between two different but related commodities.

In the previous example, gold and silver are different commodities but they are both precious metals. The spreads of soybean meal versus corn, or wheat versus corn, or oats versus corn, are examples of different commodities that are related by being animal feeds. Although it is not always the case, it is common to find that the contracts spread are possible substitutes for each other. It is this potential substitutability which gives the two contracts a relationship that can be traded by the spread trader. If wheat can be fed to animals instead of corn, the price discount of wheat to corn will be limited. Thus a long gold/short orange juice spread would not be considered an intercommodity spread for our purposes because there is no relationship between the two commodities other than color. Obviously, it is an intercommodity spread in that it is a long position in one commodity and a short position in another commodity but, because there is no fundamental relationship between commodities, it is considered two outright positions rather than an intercommodity spread.

COMMODITY VERSUS PRODUCT

A special type of intercommodity spread is the spread between a commodity and its products. The most common example is the spread between soybeans and its two products, soybean oil and soybean meal. This is usually considered to be the most complex of spreads.

Very few soybeans are used as soybeans. Nearly all soybeans are crushed into two products, soybean oil and soybean meal. Each bushel of soybeans, weighing 60 pounds, yields approximately 11 pounds of oil, 48 pounds of meal, and 1 pound of waste. The analyst must do some simple math to find the value of oil and meal per bushel of soybeans. Since oil is quoted in cents per pound, we simply multiply the oil price by 11 to get the value of bean oil in one bushel. To obtain the value of meal, the analyst multiplies the price of meal by 0.024 (0.024 is 48 pounds divided by the 2000 pounds in a ton). This converts the price of meal in dollars per ton to the value of the meal in one bushel of beans.

A soybean crusher makes a profit from the difference between the cost of buying the beans and the price of selling the products. This difference is called the *Gross Processing Margin* (GPM), or the *conversion margin*. In the futures industry the difference is commonly called the *crush margin*.

The spread created by buying soybean futures and simultaneously selling soybean oil and soybean meal futures is called the *crush spread*.

When one buys the oil and meal futures and sells the bean futures, it is called the *reverse crush* spread.

This spread is most frequently quoted in the cents per bushel that the products are worth after subtracting the value of the beans. For instance, "the May crush is running at 30¢" means that the combined value of the May contracts for the products, expressed in cents per bushel, is worth 30¢ more than the value of the May contract for beans.

BUTTERFLY SPREADS

A butterfly spread can be viewed as two interdelivery spreads combined. A butterfly spread is not the simultaneous purchase and sale of two different contracts but the simultaneous purchase and sale of three contracts. An example would be:

Short 1 April live cattle contract
Long 2 June live cattle contracts
Short 1 August live cattle contract

One should note that the middle leg of the spread has two contracts, whereas each outside leg has only one. This is because a spread usually has equal numbers of longs and shorts.

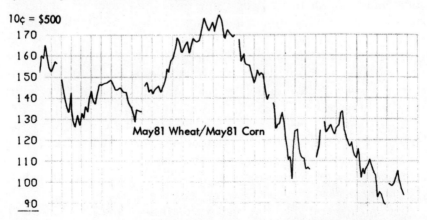

Figure 2.2   May 1981 wheat/May 1981 corn.

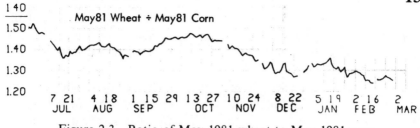

Figure 2.3   Ratio of May 1981 wheat to May 1981 corn.

A butterfly spread is typically a low volatility spread due to its structure. The fact that it is both a bull spread (long June/short August) and a bear spread (short April/long June) leads to low volatility.

INTERCOMMODITY SPREAD QUOTES

Intercommodity spreads are quoted in several different ways. If the two commodities have a similar unit of measure, for example, bushels, the spread will most likely be quoted as the difference between the two commodities in relation to their common unit. For instance, Figure 2.2 shows May wheat with the price of May corn subtracted

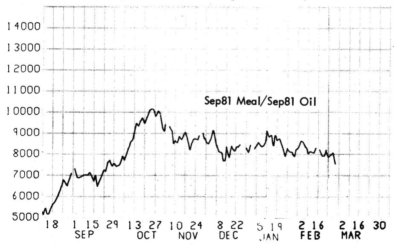

Figure 2.4   Value of September 1981 soybean meal contract minus value of September 1981 soybean oil contract.

from it. The chart is graphed as the number of cents between the commodities per bushel.

Alternatively, but less likely, the prices can be quoted as the ratio between one commodity and a second commodity. In Figure 2.3 we can see a chart of the price of May 1981 wheat divided by the price of May 1981 corn. Nonetheless, when orders are placed for execution, the common way of quoting this type of spread is the difference in cents per bushel.

The third major way that spreads are quoted is the difference between the dollar value of the contracts. In other words, the contract size times the current price of one commodity is subtracted from the contract size times the current price of a second contract. In Figure 2.4 we can see that the value of September 1981 soybean oil, subtracted from the value of September 1981 soybean meal, was worth about $10,000 in October 1980. In other words, the value of the contract of soybean meal was worth $10,000 more than the value of the contract of soybean oil. This is the most common spread that is quoted in this manner, although intercommodity currency spreads are often quoted this way also.

THREE

Why Trade Spreads?

There are a number of significant reasons why the commodity futures trader should trade spreads or at least watch them closely. A significant advantage is usually lower volatility, hence lower risk. Generally speaking, spreads move much less than outright positions. A common move in wheat is about 5¢ per day for an outright position but the wheat spreads move only about ¼¢ per day. In other words, instead of a move worth $250, as in the case of an outright position, the spread will move only about $12.50. This is not an uncommon situation in spreads, but it is particularly true in commodities that can be stored and be delivered against another contract in the future. For example, corn spreads are less volatile than hog spreads.

Many commodities are so volatile that they require constant supervision. Spreads, on the other hand, are generally sedate enough that they can be monitored once a day or less. If an account is fluctuating widely, the speculator must have more money in his or her account in order to weather the possible string of losses. Through the use of spreads, even a small trader can participate in the commodity market.

LIMITED RISK

Spreads are the only commodity investment that can have a limited risk. Because storable commodities have what are called carrying charges, there often occurs a situation where the price of a spread will rarely go past a certain level. This means that the trader can initiate a spread near that area and know the amount of risk he must bear.

LOWER RISK

Because of their hedged nature, spreads usually offer a lower risk alternative to outright positions. This is an important consideration when comparing spreads versus outright positions. The spread trader should note that there are some spreads that can have higher volatility than outright positions. An example is cattle versus hogs. Because one is trading two different commodities, it is possible that the prices of the two commodities go in opposite directions, resulting in losing or gaining money on both sides of the spread. This happens most frequently in intercommodity spreads and, to a lesser extent, in intermarket spreads.

LESS MARGIN

The exchanges allow the trader to put up a much smaller amount of margin money because of their reduced volatility. For example, a brokerage firm may require that the trader put up $1800 to buy wheat but only $300 to initiate a wheat spread. This allows the small trader to trade commodities and allows any trader to acquire a greater degree of diversification. Also, new commodity traders have an opportunity to learn about the commodity futures market while risking smaller amounts of money.

The smaller margins allow the trader to place more trades in more commodities, thus giving the trader the ability to diversify and not have all his eggs in one basket. This tends to reduce the volatility in the trader's equity. With a $10,000 account, the trader may be able to safely put on two to four outright positions but can safely initiate ten or more spread positions. This ability to spread the account risk can have an important impact on the trader's profitability. For example, a trader who is long wheat would have lost his margin money if the price of wheat dropped limit down for two consecutive days. If the wheat trader had started his account with $2000, the loss of his original margin money would mean he was no longer a wheat trader. On the other hand, it would take six consecutive losses of his margin money to turn him from a wheat spread trader to an ex-wheat spread trader. This ability to withstand more losses can contribute greatly to the trader's staying power in the marketplace.

LOCKED LIMIT DAYS

The hedged nature of most spreads provides a protection against locked limit moves. Because of political action, weather, government reports, and so on, commodity prices can move dramatically. This can create locked limit days, where prices move their daily allowed limit and no trading takes place. An outright trader with the wrong position can lose thousands of dollars before being able to liquidate the position. This can cause the trader's account to go into a deficit and force him to add money to his account. In the same circumstance, the spread trader is largely protected. Because the spread trader is both long and short in a commodity, locked limit days, though possibly anxiety producing, usually do not create deficit positions. Although the spread may move against the trader after the prices cease being locked, the loss is usually substantially less than the outright would have suffered.

It is also worth noting that because spreads are traded as spreads, not as two separate positions, they may be liquidated during lock limit days, whereas no outright positions can be liquidated. Thus it is possible that a person may wish to liquidate a spread opposite to our hypothetical trader's spread and be willing to take the other side of our trader's position. Frequently this is the only trading that takes place on locked limit days.

MORE ATTRACTIVE REWARD/RISK RATIO

A given spread may well provide a more attractive reward/risk ratio than a given outright position. For example, the value of the May/July wheat spread is largely determined by the carryover of soft red winter wheat. In the spring, the price of May wheat frequently is dominated by prospects for the new crop. This can create a situation where the outright price has fully discounted the known fundamentals and is trading in a tight trading range while the May contract is gaining or losing substantially to the July contract. Thus the May/July wheat spread can provide the opportunity for trading in wheat while the outright long or short has very little opportunity.

The determination of whether a trader should initiate a spread or an outright position is up to the individual. It should be noted, however, that the outright position must provide a higher profit in order to return the same percentage gain. In wheat, because the spread margin may be $300 and the outright margin $1800, the outright position must yield a net profit six times greater than the spread profit to yield the same return on investment.

USEFUL TO OUTRIGHT TRADER

A knowledge of spreads and spread action can be a powerful tool for the outright trader, since spread movements frequently signal the direction of the next move. For example, if the near months of corn gain relative to the far months, this generally indicates a tightening of the supply/demand situation and bull move could be in the works (this will be explained in more detail in Chapter 7). Conversely, if the nearby does not gain on the far contract during a bull move, this may be an indication that the run up is technical in nature rather than representing a fundamental change in the market. Thus the astute trader can be tipped off to a potential short or the use of a bear spread.

A close examination of spreads also may tell the trader which particular contract month she should be trading. Suppose the trader wishes to be long cattle. By examining the spreads and buying the contract that has been the strongest, the trader may get an increased return on her invested dollar. The trader who wishes to short a commodity can examine the spreads and sell the weakest option. This one simple technique should significantly improve profit performance.

FLOOR TRADERS

Traders on the floor of the commodity exchanges also gain several other advantages not always available to the general public. One of these is the ability to pay no margin for a spread position. Thus these local traders will often trade new crop/old crop spreads as a substitute for outright positions. They get almost the same action as the outright position but do not have to deposit margin. They do have to post "marked to the market" margin. This means that the trader does not have to come up with any money unless the trade is losing. Then he must come up with an amount of money equal to the loss on that position.

Local traders frequently use spreads to lock in a profit and reduce their margin requirements overnight. They will then liquidate the new leg the following morning to continue carrying their long or short position. Should the position remain profitable at the end of that day and should the trader wish to carry the outright position further, he will again put on a short position in a different contract month to lock in the profit and reduce his margin costs. It should be noted, however, that floor traders will rarely use this technique if they have a loss. They find it less expensive to merely offset the losing position and reinstate it the following morning should they desire to stay in that particular position.

It is easily seen that there are many possible advantages to using spreads. This is a powerful reason to examine spreads to gain greater insights into the marketplace. In summary, the major reasons for trading spreads are the following:

Lower margins

Less volatility

Protection against locked limit days

Sometimes better reward/risk ratio

Insight into movements of outright prices

FOUR

Why Spread Prices Change

I'd like to say that the concepts in this chapter are the final authority on the subject. Unfortunately, these are just preliminary ideas that need to be tested and analyzed further.

What follows is an attempt to present some preliminary concepts based on experience in the market. These concepts need to be examined from a more rigorous perspective in the future.

Spread price changes can be looked at as either random or nonrandom. A *random price fluctuation* is a price fluctuation which cannot be predicted. A fundamentalist using a model of sugar prices that predicts the annual average sugar price may believe that price fluctuations on a weekly or monthly basis are random; that is, they cannot be predicted. On the other hand, this fundamentalist will believe that annual price changes are not random because of his experience with his annual price model. Most traders cannot and do not try to predict where the price of a given commodity will close on a given day. They do, however, trade on the assumption that they can predict where the price will be in a week or a month. This shows that each trader, depending on level of expertise, amount of information, trading technique, and closeness to the actual trading floor, will look at price changes over different time periods as random or nonrandom.

A major theory of price behavior, the *random walk theory*, contends that there is no relationship between two prices, particularly from one day to the next. In other words, a trader cannot examine today's prices and expect to learn anything about what tomorrow's prices will be. This is sometimes referred to as *serial independence*. This simply means that each price in a series of prices is independent of the other prices in the series.

This would imply that there are no such things as seasonal or cyclical tendencies and that price trends are merely random processes. It would also imply that technical analysis, which examines only price action, has no grounding in fact. There have been a number of empirical studies, however, which imply or conclude that there are forces other than randomness in the marketplace.

A tremendous amount of time and energy has been expended in the analysis of seasonal tendencies in commodities. Books and articles by myself, Jack Grushcow, Jake Bernstein, Walt Bressert, and others have demonstrated seasonal tendencies in many commodities. These tendencies appear largely to be due to the fact that the production and consumption of many commodities occur in seasonal patterns. This constant flux of supply and demand must exert an influence on commodity prices because of the law of supply and demand.

It is easier to make a case for randomness in securities prices because of the limited interplay of supply and demand for a real object. In other words, there is supply and demand for the stock certificate, which represents ownership in the company but usually does not represent supply and demand for the company itself or its products. On the other hand, the price of cocoa does represent the supply and demand of the physical good called cocoa.

However, there are sources of randomness or unpredictability outside of the random walk theory. One such factor is the lack of floor traders in a particular market.

A *local* is a member of an exchange who trades on the floor of that particular exchange. The type of local that we are concerned with here is the *scalper*, a professional trader and exchange member who trades for his own account only. He provides much the same function as a market maker or specialist on a securities exchange. The scalper will typically buy at the bid price and sell at the asking price. It is this technique of trading in minimum fluctuations, taking small profits and small losses, which creates the heavy volume of trades necessary for proper liquidity in a marketplace.

One of the major economic functions of a scalper is to narrow the difference between the bid price and the ask price. In a commodity with no scalpers—typically a commodity with very small volume—the difference in price between the bid and ask can be very large. The trader not on the floor must accept this large bid/ask spread to induce someone to take the other side of the transaction. A scalper, by his willingness to take the other side of a transaction with only a small bid/ask spread, thus provides an economic gain for the outside trader. Commodities with large volumes tend to have many scalpers competing with each other, thus making the bid/ask spread even smaller. Heavily traded commodities, like corn or soybeans, will often have a bid/ask spread of only the minimum possible fluctuation. Some commodities with less volume will often have a bid/ask spread of four or five times the minimum fluctuation.

Some heavily traded commodities have what might be considered spread scalpers. These are floor traders who make a market by specializing in spread orders. Furthermore, within a particular pit, they will often specialize in particular spread combinations. For instance, it is usually very easy to get into and out of a July/November soybean spread but significantly harder to find someone to take the other side of an August/January bean spread. These spread scalpers provide the same advantages to the market as the outright scalpers do in outright trades. trades.

Let's look at the situation where there are no spread traders in the pit. Let's say a trader, in February 1983, wishes to initiate an August/January soybean spread. Let's further assume that there are no spread traders in the soybean pit (although this is definitely not true in the real world). The August contract, being nearer, will usually have more volume than the following January 1984 contract. If the prices of soybeans are moving strongly in one direction, the price of August beans, due to the greater volume, will tend to move faster than the January beans. The January bean contract will tend to lag behind in any price movements. To the trader looking at current commodity quotes on a video screen or ticker tape, the spread between August and January is something quite different from that seen by a spread specialist constantly trading spreads between those two months and keeping their prices in line. Thus spread prices in pits with spread scalpers tend to be more stable than spreads in commodities without spread scalpers.

This also makes it easier to get quotes on spread prices. Because of the inexactitude of video screens and ticker tapes in giving spread values from the pits, many traders will call their brokers and ask for a quote on a particular spread. The broker will come back to the trader and give him a bid and ask price on the particular spread if there is somebody making a market in that particular spread. When a pit has no spread scalpers, the account executive will often have to tell the trader that there are no quotes. This makes it more difficult for the spread trader to enter or exit positions.

Spread trading also keeps the relationship of the prices of various contracts in some degree of reasonableness. Without the spread scalper, the values between the various contract months may not represent their relative economic value. They thus become more volatile and, from the point of view of the average trader, more random.

If a large order for, say, long July wheat comes into the pit, this will have the temporary effect of driving up the price of July wheat. Without spread scalpers, July wheat would go up and, all other things being equal, the other contracts of wheat would stay the same. Because this is not economically reasonable, spread scalpers would trade spreads that force the prices back in line with each other. In this case, they may sell July wheat and buy September, thus providing a supply of July contracts and simultaneously increasing the demand for September contracts. Thus the July and September contracts would be kept in line.

As another example, some commodities, such as Chicago wheat, have more speculative interest than Kansas City wheat. Chicago will tend to fluctuate more than Kansas City wheat due to this extra speculative enthusiasm. It is spread traders who keep the relationship between Chicago and Kansas City wheat in order.

The reader should not get the impression that the only influences on the marketplace are the "random" influences of the lack of floor brokers. On the contrary, there are many more nonrandom than random influences on spread prices. Spread differentials typically represent the consensus of opinion of the market participants of the relative value of the various contracts. In fact, spreads move mainly with changing perception of commercial interests in the marketplace.

The people who spend the largest amount of time studying spreads are these commercial interests. The *commercials*, or *hedgers*, are those people who actually own or use the underlying commodity. They will look very closely at the spreads to determine their hedging and marketing strategies. As an example, if there is plenty of grain, hedgers will allow the spreads to widen toward the carrying charges. This way, they will be compensated for storing the commodity for use later. If the commercial interests need the commodity right now because of tightness of supplies and strong demand, they will bid the price of the nearby contract up higher than the far contract. When the nearby contract is higher in price than the far contract there is no incentive provided by the futures market to store the commodity. On the other hand, when the far contracts are at higher prices than the nearby contracts, hedgers can use the futures market to regain some of the costs they have to incur to carry the physical commodity. They do this by selling the far contracts in the same quantity that they own the cash commodity.

For instance, suppose a grain elevator has just bought 5000 bushels of corn for $3.00 a bushel. Suppose further that it would cost the elevator 10¢ a bushel per month to store the corn. If the futures contract expiring in three months was trading for $3.20, the elevator could sell the futures contract and recover 20¢ of the 30¢ storage costs to store the corn for the three months.

By looking at the spreads, the commercials can decide whether to roll forward their hedges or to simply put the hedge on in the appropriate month. If a hedger is holding grain in March and needs to carry it until May and the spread between the March and May contracts is at the full cost of carrying the commodity, the hedger will sell the May while holding the cash commodity. He is thus locking in compensation for storing the commodity. If, however, the market is inverted, having the nearby contracts at a higher price than the far contracts, the hedger will have a tendency to place his hedge in the exact month he wishes to be in rather than continually rolling forward from the nearby contract into each successive contract. In other words, the hedger will likely hedge in the futures month which best reimburses his carrying costs.

If December and March wheat are equal in price, the grain elevator will sell December and hope to be reimbursed for carrying charges in March. If March is selling for more than the carrying costs, the hedger will sell the March and, once again, drive the spread closer.

Commercial interests can also affect the spread price during the expiration months of the lead contract. Let's look at a very commonly occurring situation in the period immediately before a particular futures contract expires. Frequently, the nearby contract will sell at less than full carrying charges compared to the far contracts. This could induce the commercials to short the nearby and purchase a far month. They can then deliver their cash commodity from their inventories with the intention of taking delivery in the far month.

For example, commercials may sell the March contract and buy the May contract if the March is selling for less than full carrying charges. They would then deliver against their short March and stand for delivery on their long May contract. This enables the commercial to maintain control over the commodity during the period from March to May without having to pay the full carrying costs. Obviously, commercials who need the commodity in April will not execute this strategy because they will not be able to regain the actual cash commodity until the May contract expires.

It should be noted that if many commercials followed this strategy, the nearby contract would have a tendency to move closer to full carrying charges. Commercial selling can induce additional selling from speculators moving out of their long positions in the nearby contract. This can have further depressing action on the nearby contract in relationship to the far contract as many of the speculators will roll out of their longs in the nearby into longs in the far. Many of them do this by putting in a spread order to sell the nearby and buy the far.

This pressure in the nearby future can cause it to go to nearly full carrying charges. Some commercial interests may find it profitable to buy back their shorts in the nearby and cover their longs in the far. They may, in fact, go further and sell the far contract in order to lock in this newly found reimbursement of carrying charges. This is an example of the type of machinations commercial firms will go through in a very short time period. They will often do this for small spread differentials because their transaction costs are small if they are members of the exchange. Thus the large grain companies, such as Garnac, Continental Grain, and Bunge, are major participants in the spread market.

One reason spreads rarely go to 100% of full carry is that speculators will step into the market, put on the spread, and get an essentially risk-free trade. Their only risk is that the carrying charges will change during the time that they are in the trade.

Spreads also change because supply and demand can be different at different times in the future. The commodities market will try to discount the future in terms of the supply and demand differences. For example, the highest production of hogs tends to be in the fall, but the highest demand tends to be in the summer, so hog futures prices tend to be higher in the summer than in the fall. It is common to see the April hog contract below the August contract, which is also above the October contract. This is a typical formation in the meat markets because of the relative differences in supply and demand throughout the year.

This supply/demand imbalance creates seasonal spread opportunities in the hogs. Because the supply tends to get smaller while the demand is strengthening, the June contract tends to gain on the following October contract through the first half of the year.

Spreads can also change simply due to a change in the carrying charges. This will be explained in detail in Chapter 6.

We have examined a number of explanations of why spreads move in different situations. This is by no means an exhaustive examination but merely an effort to show the trader that there are many reasons for spread price action.

FIVE

Carrying Charges

Carrying charges occupy an important place in spread trading. They permeate the analysis of many commodities. No matter what type of analysis is being used, the trader must be cognizant of carrying charges. Carrying charges can be used to delineate risk as well as to provide profit opportunities.

Suppose a person decided, for whatever reason, to buy 5,000 bushels of corn on September 1 and carry (or hold or store) it until December first. He would have to pay several costs to carry the corn: storage for the corn; insurance against loss or damage; perhaps interest on a loan if he borrowed the money to buy the corn. These costs—storage, insurance, and financing—are the carrying charges. Carrying charges are the cost of carrying a commodity for a particular period of time.

Carrying charges can be different for different people for the same commodity. If a person or company owned a corn bin that was built and paid for 20 years ago, the storage costs could be considered negligible. Storing the corn at a public elevator would cost much more.

Some people or companies are in a position to borrow money less expensively than other people or companies. A very large company may be able to borrow money at less than the prime rate, whereas a smaller company may have to pay something above the prime rate.

It can be seen that the cost of carry is variable. Nonetheless, an industry standard exists. Full carrying charges are considered to be the cost of storage and insurance at a public warehouse and financing at the prime rate plus 1%.

29

It is important to realize that a commodity can be held for less than the commonly accepted full carry cost. A commercial cash corn firm may charge customers 4.2¢ per bushel per month to store the corn, but the firm's actual cost may only be 3¢ per bushel per month. The commercial firm's carrying charge can therefore be less than its clients. This is one reason why grain spreads rarely reach the commonly accepted full carrying charges.

The common carrying charges mentioned by spread market participants should therefore be considered as only a rule of thumb. The following discussion mentions carrying charges as of this writing (October 1981) but should be confirmed. Any brokerage house will be able to provide current carrying charges.

Carrying charges affect the futures market. The carrying charges for futures are identical to those in the cash market with the minor additional cost of delivery and redelivery.

Carrying charges in the futures market apply only to commodities which are storable, deliverable, and redeliverable. The trader must be able to take delivery of a commodity, store it until the next futures contract expires, and deliver it against that contract.

Commodities which are easily storable and redeliverable include:

Wheat	Cocoa
Corn	Coffee
Oats	Copper
Soybeans	Silver
Soybean oil	Gold
Cotton	Platinum
Orange juice	Plywood

Commodities which are not storable and cannot be redelivered and hence do not have carrying charges include:

Live cattle
Live hogs
Feeder cattle

There are commodities that do not quite fall into these two neat categories. They include:

Pork bellies	Potatoes
Sugar	Currencies
Lumber	Interest rates
Soybean meal	

Let's take a closer look at some of these unusual commodities. The commodities that we don't talk about here will be covered later in the book in more detail.

UNUSUAL COMMODITIES

Pork Bellies

The pork belly futures contract is for frozen pork bellies which are, of course, storable. Still, they have a unique delivery situation. There are contracts for pork bellies for the months of February, March, May, July, and August. Bellies may be redelivered only against a contract that expires in the same calendar year. In other words, one cannot take delivery of August 1982 bellies and redeliver them against the February 1983 contract. The trader, however, could take delivery of the February 1982 bellies and redeliver against the March 1982, May 1982, or August 1982 contracts.

Hog slaughter is at its peak in the October to May period. Typically, more bellies are produced during that period than are consumed. The excess production is frozen and becomes the basis of the frozen pork belly contract. During the months of May through September, there is usually less belly production than demand. Thus the bellies frozen during October to May are sold to fill the demand.

Frozen pork bellies are actually somewhat perishable. The longer they are frozen the more they shrink and become susceptible to such damage as freezer burns and bruises. The older frozen bellies are used before the new batch of fresh bellies is frozen during the October to May period. It is because of this waxing and waning of stocks and downgrading of quality that bellies are not delivered against a contract from one calendar year to another.

Pork belly contracts in the same calendar year do have carrying charges. In addition to the storage, insurance, and finance charges, bellies also have an initial freezing charge. Currently, this charge is

.53¢ per pound. There is also a handling charge of 1.78¢ per pound. This is added to the current storage and insurance charge of .47¢ per month in Chicago warehouses plus the normal finance charges.

There is, however, an exception to the charges outlined in the preceding paragraph. The freezing and handling charges are added to the futures market carrying charges in spreads that have February as one of the two months. It is assumed that the freezing and handling charges will have been paid by the expiration of the February contract and do not have to be paid by anyone delivering or redelivering on contracts that expire after February. Carrying charges between all months but February include only the usual storage, insurance, and financing charges.

Traders should note that the August belly contract will often sell at a discount to the preceding contracts in the current crop year. Each successive contract in a year usually is higher in price than the preceding contract with the exception of the August contract. The July contract will nearly always sell at a premium to the August. This is because of the natural deterioration of the frozen bellies. The pork belly in August will be in worse condition than in preceding months.

Sugar

Sugar is somewhat unusual in that carrying charges could theoretically apply but, as a practical matter, they don't enter the picture. The world sugar contract calls for delivery of types of raw sugar from a port in the country of origin or, in the case of a landlocked country, at the berth or anchorage in the usual port free on board and stowed in bulk. In other words, the sugar could be delivered just about anywhere in the world except the United States.

The trader taking delivery may have to pay demurrage, storage, and food and salaries for a bunch of sailors in Indonesia! May I be so bold as to suggest that trying to assign carrying charges might be difficult. Although a trader could assume some theoretical worst case, it is not worth the effort. The sugar market just ignores the existence of carrying charges because of the impracticality of assigning them.

Lumber

It would seem at first glance that lumber would be a commodity with carrying charges. However, lumber delivered in one month cannot be redelivered against a contract in the future. The current contract states that the lumber be delivered on rail at the millsite. This apparently makes it difficult for anyone but one of the certified mills to deliver against a contract. This market treats lumber as having no limits to the amount a far contract can go over a near.

Soybean Meal

Soybean meal is a perishable commodity but still has carrying charges. When one takes delivery of soybean meal, one is not taking delivery of the actual meal but of a certificate which gives one the right to some actual soybean meal stored at a soybean processor's plant. Soybean meal has a life of about two to three months before going bad. This limits the ability to deliver against a future contract. The certificate, on the other hand, can be delivered against any contract up to six months after taking delivery. The trader holds the certificate, not the actual meal, for the six months.

Unfortunately for the trader, the soybean processor charges the trader carrying charges for each month that the trader holds the certificate. It is this mechanism which creates the carrying charges in a perishable commodity.

STORAGE AND INSURANCE

Storage and insurance charges change occasionally, and spreaders should be alert for such changes. Traders should also note that storage charges vary from one warehouse to another. The charges listed below are the charges that are the commonly accepted costs to carry. As this was written the storage and insurance charges for the storable and redeliverable commodities were:

Commodity	Monthly Storage and Insurance
Wheat	4.2¢ per bushel
Kansas City wheat	3.8¢ per bushel
Corn	4.2¢ per bushel
Oats	4.2¢ per bushel
Soybeans	4.2¢ per bushel

Commodity	Monthly Storage and Insurance
Soybean oil	9 points per pound or $54 per contract
Cotton	25 points per pound or $125 per contract
Plywood	65 points per 1,000 square feet or $49 per contract
Gold	2 points per ounce or $2 per contract
Platinum	2 points per ounce or $2 per contract
Silver	15 points per ounce or $7.50 per contract
Copper	$30 per contract
Orange juice	29¢ per hundredweight
Coffee	40¢ per bag
Cocoa	42¢ per bag

FINANCING COSTS

Financing costs make up the greatest portion of carrying charges. It is always assumed that the money necessary to buy and hold the cash commodity is borrowed.

Even when the money is not borrowed, there is a cost to use it. The user loses the opportunity to use the money in other investments. Even though this opportunity cost is usually less than the cost of borrowing, the latter is considered the financing cost.

The borrowing cost used for calculating carrying charges is the prime rate plus an additional 1%. If the prime rate is 20%, the financing cost would be 21%. This simulates the cost to most businesses in the position of carrying the cash commodity.

With March copper at 70¢ and the prime rate at 18%, it would cost 6.65¢ to finance the copper until September. Half the finance costs are charged because it is six months from March to September. The interest rate used would be 18% plus 1% or 19%. This would be divided in half, because of the six-month time span, and multiplied by the price of copper. Thus 9.5% times 70¢ equals 6.65¢. Storage and insurance would be extra.

Costs must always be adjusted by the number of months the commodity would be carried. If the commodity will be carried 12 months, then use the prime rate plus 1%. If the commodity will be carried for less or more than one year, the finance cost must be adjusted. To adjust the finance costs, determine the number of months the commodity will be carried, find that number in Table 5.1, and multiply the adjustment factor times the prime rate plus 1%.

There is sometimes confusion as to how many months there are between futures contracts. For instance, some people contend that traders should count the first month in the spread, so that March to September would count as seven months. The correct way, however,

Table 5.1   Finance Cost Adjustment Factor

Months	Adjustment Factor
1	.0833
2	.1667
3	.2500
4	.3333
5	.4167
6	.5000
7	.5833
8	.6667
9	.7500
10	.8333
11	.9167
12	1.0000
13	1.0833
14	1.1667
15	1.2500
16	1.3333
17	1.4167
18	1.5000
19	1.5833
20	1.6667
21	1.7500
22	1.8333
23	2.0000

is to assume six months from March to September. This is counting from the typical first delivery day in March, March 1, to the typical first delivery day in September, September 1. This is in spite of the fact that the trader could conceivably take delivery on the first of March and not tender the commodity for delivery until the third week in September. This would be a total of six and three quarters months.

As a practical matter, this is not an issue. On most commodity exchanges, the earliest a trader could take delivery would be on the first of the month. He doesn't know exactly when he will be delivered to, but he knows it won't be any sooner than the first.

Typically, the holder of the short position has the option of when to deliver during the delivery period. The trader could deliver on the first delivery day or carry the contract to the last delivery day. If the trader wishes to minimize carrying cost, he will deliver on the first delivery day.

The trader now knows that he will have to carry the commodity for six months or less. It can be less, because it is possible that he will not be delivered to until sometime after the nearby month's first delivery day. In fact, he may not be delivered to until the last delivery day. The point is simply that the trader will have to carry the commodity beyond six months only if he decides to.

Nonetheless, the industry standard is to consider the carrying period as stretching from the first day of the nearby contract's delivery month to the first day of the far contract's delivery month.

Because the commodity may be carried farther than the first delivery day, in a very bearish market, full carrying charges may reflect the cost of carry to the last delivery day, not the first.

This will happen when conditions are so bearish that very high carrying charges may be necessary to induce cash commodity holders to carry their stocks for as long as possible. This is one reason why spreads, in rare circumstances, trade above their apparent carrying charges.

CARRYING CHARGE MARKETS

A market where the back months are priced higher than the near months is called a carrying charge market. Figure 5.1 shows wheat contract prices in a carrying charge market. Table 5.2 presents full

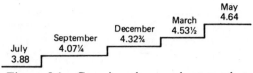

Figure 5.1   Carrying charge wheat market.

carrying charges for each possible spread at the time this chart was constructed (June 23, 1981).

The actual spreads were therefore at the percentages of full carry given in Table 5.3. It is apparent that spreads within one commodity, one market, and one crop year can fall within a large range of percentage of full carry. In this example, spreads ranged from a low of 44% to a high of 81% of full carry.

The percentage of full carry the spreads represent gives the spreader a lot of useful information. If the spreader wanted to be bull spread he would have more confidence in the bull spread that was at 81% of full carry than the one at 44%, all other things being equal. Conversely, the bear spreader would be more comfortable bear spreading March/May rather than July/December.

Traders should not think that they only need to find the spread at the greatest or least percentage of full carry. There can be reasons for the divergence in percentage of full carry. The trader must examine the fundamentals to ensure that the reasons for the divergence may

Table 5.2   Wheat Carrying Changes

Spread	Full Carrying Charges (Cents)
July/September	22
July/December	55
July/March	88
July/May	110
September/December	34
September/March	68
September/May	91
December/March	35
December/May	59
March/May	24

Table 5.3 Wheat Spreads—Percentage of Full Carry

Spread	Spread Value (Cents)	Percentage of Full Carry
July/September	15¼	69
July/December	44¾	81
July/March	65½	74
July/May	76	69
September/December	25½	75
September/March	46¼	68
September/May	56¾	62
December/March	20¾	59
December/May	31¼	53
March/May	10½	44

not work against the proposed spread. For example, the spread at 81% of full carry could be that close to full carry because the market expects low exports because of the winter closing of the Great Lakes. Perhaps a bullish bias is built into the back spreads because the market is less sure that the situation will be as bearish in the far future as it is in the near future.

The trader who does not trade spreads will still find this information useful. The speculator, seeking a profit from the short side, should short the far contract that represents the closest to full carry. In the wheat example above, December wheat was the contract that was closest to full carry compared to the contracts preceding it. The short speculator (not in stature but in position) will tend to make additional profits if wheat declines in price. Should wheat rally, however, our short speculator would likely lose more money in the short December position. This is because full carrying charges rise and fall partially in response to a rise or fall in the absolute price of the underlying commodity. The carrying charges on wheat prices at $3.00 a bushel will be less than the carrying charges at $4.00 a bushel because of smaller financing charges. At 20% interest rates, it should cost 6.7¢ per month to finance $4.00 wheat but only 5¢ per month to finance $3.00 wheat.

Table 5.4 presents an example of the effect of a $1.00 per bushel decline in September wheat on the price of the following March contract of wheat. This change in the price of the March contract will

Table 5.4   Effect of Decline in Price

	Before	After
Interest rate	20%	20%
September wheat price per bushel	$4.00	$3.00
Storage cost	.25	.25
Financing cost	.40	+ .30
Full carry	.65	.55
	× .80	× .80
	.52	.44
March wheat	$4.52	$4.44

change the spread relationship between the March and September contracts, if all other factors are ignored, and the September/March wheat spread stays at 80% of full carry. The spread has moved 8¢ for no other reason than that the outright price of wheat dropped a dollar. The spread would have moved in the opposite direction had the price of September wheat rallied instead of slumped. Therefore, the bearish speculator would have picked up an additional 8¢ a bushel shorting the March rather than the September.

INVERTED MARKETS

An inverted market is a market in which the near contracts sell for more than the far contracts. This occurs in storable and redeliverable commodities when there is an exceptional demand for the commodity in the face of a tightness in supply. An example of an inverted market is seen in Figure 5.2.

In a nonstorable commodity, an inverted market simply means that the market has ascertained that the supply/demand situation is more bullish in the near contracts than in the far.

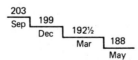

Figure 5.2   Inverted oat market.

THE MEANING OF INVERTED OR CARRYING CHARGE MARKETS

A market with carrying charges is offering the carrying charges as an inducement to carry the cash commodity into the future. The closer the spread is to full carry, the greater the inducement is to carry the cash commodity. In effect, the market is bidding a higher price for the commodity in the future than now. It may be advantageous for a cash merchant to sell his corn in the March futures at $3.25 than to sell it in the cash market now, in December, at $3.00. The greater the spread between the future price and the current price, the greater the quantity of corn will be offered in the future.

Notice that only the most bearish situation could get the spread to full carrying charges. Full carrying charges are a message from the market to the holder of the cash commodity to store the commodity as long as possible.

The cash holder can sell a futures contract in the future which will fully reimburse the holder for the carrying charges. Thus the carrying charges represent what the market is willing to pay someone to store the commodity. As the price differential moves away from full carry there becomes less incentive for someone to carry the commodity and more incentive to sell it on the spot market.

When spreads invert, with the nearby contracts trading for higher prices than the far contracts, the market is giving an incentive to the cash commodity holder to not store the commodity but to sell it on the spot market as soon as possible. The market may be saying, "Here, we'll give you $2.03 a bushel for your oats now but only $1.90 a bushel if you wait until March to sell them." The incentive to sell them now is obvious.

The cash commodity holder might not want to sell immediately, however, if it appears that the price will rise. The oat owner who was only offered $1.90 a bushel for March oats in the futures market may believe oats will actually be selling for $2.25 a bushel when March rolls around. This belief might provide enough incentive to hold the oats rather than to sell them now. Nonetheless, by not selling the oats at the current spot price of $2.03, this oat owner is not only speculating on a price rise but is also losing the opportunity to use the cash in other ways. For instance, the oat owner could sell the oats now for $2.03 and put the money in Treasury Bills (if he sold enough oats).

Because of this option, he must face the possibility that his oats will not rise in price enough to yield the same as his investment in Treasury Bills.

An inverted market thus provides a negative inducement to hold the commodity. It is sometimes called negative carrying charges when a market is inverted. One can consider this as a negative return for holding inventories. However negtive this may appear to the cash commodity holder, it is a useful tool for speculators.

When spreads in storable commodities invert, there is a tightness in the supply/demand situation. The spread trader can capitalize on this situation by initiating bull spreads.

SPREADS RARELY GO TO FULL CARRY

Carrying charges rarely go to full carry for two reasons. First, if a spread were to trade at full carry, speculators would step in and have a trade with very little risk. The only risk would be that the carrying charges widen. Because the market usually doesn't consider this much of a risk, the spreads rarely get to full carry. As the spread gets closer to full carry and has less risk, more traders will buy the spread (buy the nearby contract and sell the far contract) until the spread reaches a point where buying pressure halts the spread from moving closer to full carry. This buying of the near contract and selling of the far contract exerts a pressure to move the spreads away from full carry and occurs before the spreads reach full carry.

Second, the full carrying charges represent the theoretical costs. A large commercial interest may not have to pay the full carrying costs. It is conceivable that a commercial will not borrow the money necessary to carry the inventory. Perhaps the commercial will simply carry the inventory rather than selling it and putting the proceeds in the bank. Storage costs are usually lower for commercial interests than for individuals. The costs outlined above were the price that the commercials are charging their customers. Since we can presume that they are making a profit, their own costs must be lower. It is therefore quite possible for a commercial to consider carrying charges to be significantly lower than the theoretical full carry. It is probable that commercials would be locking in a profit if they were to sell futures contracts at theoretical full carry.

A BULLISH SIGNAL

The outright trader can also find the inversion of spreads an important indicator. The supply/demand tightness will sometimes first become known by the nearby contracts gaining on the far, even to the point of inverting. This should alert the outright trader to the potential profits on the long side.

The outright trader can also see that a current supply/demand tightness is easing when an inverted market returns to a carrying charge market. Similarly, some major market tops have been indicated by inverted spreads failing to make new highs as the price moves into new high ground.

The moving of the spread price from carrying charge to inverted and back again is a powerful indicator. The trader, however, should not blindly buy a commodity every time the market inverts. She should use other trading tools, be they fundamental or technical, to supplement the spread action's signal with a specific trading plan.

It is wise to remember that prices can drop during periods of supply/demand tightness. It is possible that the market has not yet noticed the tightness.

On the other hand, the market may have noticed the prospective tightness before it occurs and the price moved upward to discount the predicted tightness. Often the price will shoot higher than the expected tightness would suggest.

When the actual tightness finally occurs, the price may actually be dropping. The spreads may be showing tightening of the supply/demand situation but the outright price may be showing an apparent easing. This situation occurred in 1971 in the cotton market, as can be seen in Figure 5.3.

Most of the time, this is not what happens. The spreads tighten due to supply/demand tightness and the outright price shoots up. Often the spread will lead the outright but usually the spread will move with the outright. This situation can be seen in Figure 5.3 in 1973/1974.

There is another reason for the outright trader to watch spreads. Watching spreads can usually tip off the trader to whether a price movement is based on funadmentals or technicals. There are many reasons for spread differences to move. The most common reason for significant spread movements is the tightening and easing of supply

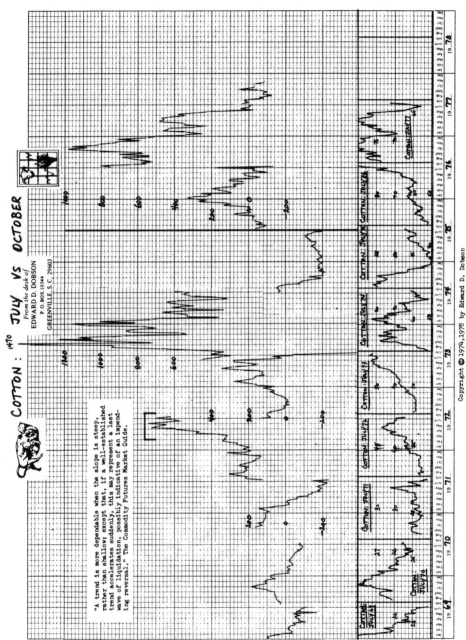

COTTON : 14/10 JULY vs OCTOBER

From the desk of
EDWARD D. DOBSON
P O BOX 10344
GREENVILLE, S. C. 29603

"A trend is more dependable when the slope is steep, rather than shallow; except that, if a well-established trend accelerates suddenly, this may represent a last wave of liquidation, possibly indicative of an impending reversal." The Commodity Futures Market Guide.

C-20

Copyright © 1974,1978 by Edward D. Dobson

Figure 5.3 July/October cotton spread history.

43

and demand. Thus if the outrights are rallying and the near contracts are gaining on the far contracts, we can say that the rally is probably based on fundamentals, that is, a change from an easier supply/demand situation to a tighter situation. Fundamentally oriented price movements tend to be stronger and longer. The outright trader may want to buy rallies which are accompanied by tightening spreads but sell rallies that have flat spreads or, even better, spreads that are going to greater carrying charges. When the outright's price is slumping, the trader would be looking for spreads to be getting closer to carrying charges to confirm the bear move. Tightening spreads would tell our trader that the price move may be short lived. The trader must be alert, however, to the possibility that the tightening is only the result of a lowering of financing charges. Chapter 6 examines changes in the carrying charges in more detail.

SIX

Carrying Charge Spreads

Carrying charges have more uses than being helpful in delineating risk. There are several ways to trade spreads that utilize carrying charges. Their combination of low risk, low margins, and relative ease of analysis make them an attractive commodity investment.

Carrying charge spreads are particularly suitable for the novice trader. Most beginning traders start their trading careers by losing money as they learn. Carrying charge spreads serve the useful purpose of involving the trader in actual trading with a relatively small investment and limited losses. Of course, after reading this book the trader should have enough ammunition to become a profitable trader right away.

FULL CARRY SPREADS

A full carry spread is a spread initiated at or near full carry. Anything over 70% of full carry is considered to be near full carry. Although the risk is minimal, the profit potential is large.

Richard L. Meyer's *Application and Analysis of Pork Belly Spreads* (published by the Chicago Mercantile Exchange) examines several strategies of trading pork belly spreads. Although each strategy is different, they all are concerned with buying pork belly spreads at various percentages of full carry.

45

Meyer tested the various strategies on pork belly prices from 1964 to 1971. He found that a strategy of buying pork belly spreads at any percentage of full carry would have been a profitable strategy during the years he studied. The most amazing thing he discovered was that a trader would never have lost money on a pork belly spread if it had been placed at 60% of full carry or greater!

This illustrates exactly what was mentioned earlier—that carrying charge spreads have less risk than most commodity investments and yet contain enough profit potential to make them attractive.

Let's look at an example of a full carry spread. It's early July. A record-breaking wheat crop is being harvested. Full carry on the September/December wheat spread is 34¢. It is currently trading at 30¢ premium the December. This is 88.2% of full carry. Unless carrying charges widen, the risk is 4¢ plus commissions.

The trader could have put the spread on before it got to 30¢ premium the December. Alternately, he could wait until it gets even closer to full carry. His decision can be based on fundamental or technical reasons. Money management can also be a deciding factor. Is the trader able and willing to risk 10¢? 5¢? 4¢? Perhaps he is willing to lose a total of 8 cents but wants to put on two spreads, risking 4¢ each.

After putting the spread on at 30¢ premium the December he waits for something to happen. It could be that the trader has no idea about what could happen that would make the spread profitable. He figures that he has two months for something or anything to happen. Perhaps the trader has very specific reasons for thinking that the September contract will gain on the December. The technician may see strong support at 31¢ premium the December or he may have seen an inverse head and shoulders. The fundamentalist may be looking for exports to be strong, perhaps because of a big sale to the Russians. He may see that a new government program will cause the September to gain on the December.

Whatever the reason, he expects to make money when the near contract gains on the far. At the same time, he has essentially predetermined his risk. The spread, initiated at 30¢ premium December, cannot go beyond 34¢ premium December unless the carrying charges increase.

LIMITED RISK

The trader will seldom be able to put on a spread at full carry. The spread will most often be initiated near full carry. The risk is limited by the difference between the entry price and full carry. This is commonly called a limited risk spread. It is basically the only limited risk trading opportunity in commodities.

Actually, the risk is theoretically not limited. The carrying charges could widen considerably, thus adding to the so-called limited risk. Later in this chapter we examine spreads that are initiated to profit from changes in carrying charges.

Even though carrying charges could widen considerably, as a practical matter, the widening is usually not of very much importance. There have been some exceptions, such as gold spreads in 1979/1980, but in general carrying charges change slowly. The section below that discusses carrying charge change spreads will point out those commodities whose spreads are particularly susceptible to changes in carrying charges.

Most full, or nearly full carrying charge spreads are done in the grains. Since carrying charges change slowly in the grains, they are the most suitable for these types of spread. Pork bellies, soybean meal, soybean oil, cocoa, coffee, cotton, orange juice, plywood, and sometimes copper are also suitable for full carry spreads.

SIMPLE TO TRADE

Full carry spreads are the easiest type of spread to trade. All the trader need do is find out the full carry in a particular commodity and she is in business. When the spread price moves to a point that has sufficiently limited the risk, say 80% of full carry, the trader merely puts on the trade. She then carries it until delivery month or to a point where profits are sufficient to compensate for the risk. Of course, she may have other fundamental or technical reasons for wanting to liquidate a trade but, at a minimum, she only has to follow the simple policy given in the preceding sentence.

Readers may question the desirability of putting on a bull spread in the midst of a bearish fundamental situation. The major risk that the trader has is that nothing will happen and that the trader will lose commissions. The trader is really betting that something will happen before the expiration of the first contract. That "something" could be dramatically increased foreign or domestic demand, currency fluctuation, weather problems, disease, or new government actions. All of these things could cause the spread to move in the direction the trader wants. He is willing to hold the position because the risk is low. He carries the position waiting for something to happen.

Another possible tactic for full carry spreads is to keep track of the various spreads and their relationship to full carry but to invest in the spread only when it starts to move away from full carry. This approach has the advantage of not putting the trader in a trade which ends up looking like a dead log until expiration. The trader may save margin money and commissions, not to mention the alleviation of potential boredom.

On the other hand, the trader will have to pay a premium to get into the trade because it has already started to move away from full carry. The speculator may be willing to pay this premium in exchange for increased chances of success. There is no doubt that prices could begin to move away from full carry, reverse course, and move back toward full carry. The trader will nevertheless have increased trade odds by waiting for the move away from full carry. The trader may have been able to identify the reasons behind the move away from full carry and come to some opinion of its validity.

Another tactic is to initiate one spread when the price gets as low as the trader thinks it will go, or close enough to full carry to be of acceptable risk, and to initiate a second spread when the spread price begins to move away from full carry. This is a happy medium between the two strategies outlined above. It combines both the strengths and the weaknesses of the two approaches.

The full carry spread is a particularly interesting proposition if it can be placed in months that are very deferred. In other words, in January 1982 the trader should be looking to put on January 1983/ March 1983 soybean spreads or even March 1983/May 1983 bean spreads. These would enable the trader to have a significantly longer period of time for something to happen. This increases the chance of profit for the trader. Drawbacks include the boredom factor, tying up capital for longer periods of time, and the relative illiquidity of the deferred months.

It is sometimes hard to obtain a good execution on spreads that are that far in the future. The patient trader can put in a limit order on the spread waiting for the spread price to come to the level the trader seeks. This is better than trying to chase the market using a market spread order. Because of the thin liquidity in the far months a market order could be an expensive proposition.

The problem with spreads in the far months is not the entry but the exit. Suppose a trader gets into a far month carrying charge spread and it begins to move closer to full carry. If the spread trader is in a position to carry the loss, then the exit problem in far months is nonexistent. But what if, for some reason, the trader wants to bail out of his spread? If he has the time, placing limit orders will work fine. If he is in a hurry, a market order will be costly.

Thus a disadvantage of deferred carrying charge spreads is the difficulty of quick exit. Some traders may find the numerous opportunities in distant spreads to be worth the risk.

A CHANGE IN CARRYING CHARGES

It is clear that a full carry spread contains the least risk of all commodity trades. Generally speaking, the major worry is that the carrying charges themselves will change.

Storage and insurance charges can change and typically do every few years. Although the storage and insurance charges outlined in the last chapter were valid as this was being written, the reader should check with a broker to obtain the latest charges.

The most likely loss possibility is that the spread price goes nowhere. Perhaps the market fundamentals are so bearish that the price remains locked in the low volatility range. The spreader has lost commissions on the trade as well as the opportunity to use the margin money in another trade.

On the other hand, a trader could take excess margin money in his account and place it in full carry spreads if any are available. This gives him the opportunity for gain but limits the risk. Instead of money lying unproductive in an account, it is working in a potentially profitable trade. Even the trader who usually keeps his margin money in Treasury Bills may find it to his advantage to place some of his capital into low-risk carrying charge spreads.

One potential hazard to the profitability of full carry spreads is a price rally due to speculative technical reasons. As the outright price rallies, the carrying charges widen because of the increased cost of financing the now higher priced spread. If the bull market was based on a tightening of supply and demand, the spread would move away from full carry. The spreader would be holding a profitable position.

If the price of a September corn contract rises $3.00 to $3.50 during a time of 16% interest rates, the financing charge would rise from 12¢ to 14¢ for the period September to December. The holder of a long September/short December corn spread would probably have the spread move against him the 2¢ in a technical rally. This would be necessary to keep the spread at the same percentage of full carry.

Recently, another hazard has become more likely. Interest rates have gyrated wildly, causing carrying charges to change more than they have in the past. As interest rates increase, the financing charges also increase, causing the carrying charges to increase, potentially leading to an unprofitable situation for the full carry spreader.

An increase from 12% to 16% in the prime rate will increase the financing charge and hence the carrying charges. The September/December corn spread, with September corn at $3.00, will have had 3¢ added to its carrying charges. Sometimes the effects of the various carrying charge factors cancel each other out. If interest rates are going in one direction and the outright commodity price is going in the other direction, the effects on the carrying charges can be partly or totally offset. If September corn went from $3.50 to $3.00 a bushel while the prime rate moved from 12% to 16%, the net effect would be to increase the carrying charges of the September/December corn spread by the grand sum of 1¢ The interest rate movement increased the carrying charges by 3¢ while the price decline reduced the carrying charges by 2¢ for the net change of 1 cent.

This changing of the full carry is a recent problem. Prior to the last few years, commodity prices were low and interest rates changed very slowly. We now have commodity prices several times higher than they were ten years ago. The change in interest rates in six months now is greater than the prime rate was ten years ago. We are obviously in a new ball game.

The point is that the simple carrying charge of the past must now be examined more closely in light of the more volatile nature of carrying charges. We have focused mainly on the potential negative effects the changes have on the full carry spreads. But these changes have also created additional opportunities.

CARRYING CHARGE CHANGE SPREADS

What was a disadvantage when trading full carry spreads will become an advantage when trading the carrying charge change spread. A carrying charge change spread is a spread which seeks to profit from a change in carrying charges. Since it is difficult to predict when changes will occur in storage and insurance costs, carrying charge change spreads concentrate on changes in interest rates and absolute price levels.

For example, storage and insurance account for only $2.00 per contract per month for gold, whereas interest charges account for hundreds of dollars per month. If gold is selling for $400.00 per ounce and the financing interest cost is 12% per year, the financing cost per month is $4.00 ($400.00 $\times$ 12% = $48.00, which, divided by 12 months, equals $4.00 per month or 400 points per month). Because the interest costs are 400 points per month compared with 2 points per month storage and insurance, the gold spreader can, for all practical purposes, ignore storage and insurance costs.

Gold is not an abberation because it has small storage and insurance costs. Several other commodities are similar in that the carrying charges are composed mainly of interest rate costs. At 12% interest rates, it costs 6¢ interest to carry a bushel of $6.00 soybeans compared with 4.2¢ for storage and insurance.

Because carrying charges are dominated by interest rates, the spread trader must have an opinion on the future direction of interest rates. Thus carrying charge change spreads are mainly a way of trading a change in interest rates. It it true that the trader may wish to simply trade Treasury Bond or Treasury Bill futures instead of carrying charge change spreads. He may even prefer to trade spreads in the Treasury Bond and Treasury Bill futures.

Bond and bill futures may be the best way to speculate on interest rates (we will examine the interest rate futures spreads later). There are reasons, however, for speculating on carrying charge changes in commodities rather than the interest rate futures. Perhaps the risk is lower. Perhaps the liquidity is greater. Perhaps there are secondary reasons to expect a change in a spread other than a change in interest rates. Whatever the reason, it is worth noting that traders utilized carrying charge change spreads to profit from interest rate changes for years before interest futures existed.

Commodities which are in extremely bearish conditions and have moved toward full carry also will have their spreads change simply because of the change in carry charges. This might include soybeans, corn, pork bellies, and other storable commodities. Typically, though, these commodities will not be close enough to full carry so that a change in interest rates will affect their spreads in a significant way. Other factors will dominate the changes in their spreads.

Gold, silver, and platinum have been the usual commodities used in carrying charge change spreads. This is simply because the precious metals' carrying charges are virtually all financing costs and are dominated by interest rate changes.

It is rare for precious metal spreads to move for some reason other than changes is their carrying charges. The absolute price level and the current interest rates are the major motivating factors behind spread movements.

Occasionally a rumor will move through the silver pits that a short squeeze is imminent. This seems to happen because occasionally the open interest in the expiring month in silver is many times larger than the deliverable stocks even up to first notice day. This prospective short squeeze will push the nearby contract over the next forward contract by a few cents. This is an isolated instance of another factor moving a precious metals spread.

IMPLIED YIELDS

Carrying charges can be turned on their heads and looked at as yields on an investment. Since financing costs are the bulk of the costs in some commodities, particularly the precious metals, a person could collect the financing charges instead of paying them.

Here's how it works. Gold is selling for $408 an ounce and a trader has about $40,000 to invest. She seeks a high return with low risk (don't we all). She looks in the paper and sees that a gold contract for delivery one year in the future is trading at $472.

She buys 100 ounces of cash gold for $408 per ounce and simultaneously sells a 100-ounce contract of gold for delivery one year in the future at $472 an ounce. As far as the gold market is concerned she is not flat. She is long 100 ounces of cash gold and short 100 ounces of future delivery gold. But she has bought the gold at $408 and, in effect, presold it at $472. The difference between the buying and selling prices, $64, is the profit.

It is also her return on investment. It is the same as if she had placed $408 in a time deposit and was guaranteed by the bank that the $408 would grow to $472. In either case, the investment yields 15.7% per annum. (The $64 profit divided by the initial investment of $408 is 0.157 or 15.7%.)

The investor may prefer to get long the nearby and take delivery rather than buy in the cash market. This gives the investor the option of redelivering against her short position.

Also, the trader must realize that she may be required to post additional margin if the price of gold rallies. As the price of gold rallies, the investor will find she has a losing position in her short gold position. Her net position is flat. That is, her loss in the short futures is made up in the long cash position. Nonetheless, she will have to find additional cash to post as margin for the futures position. She may not use her cash gold for margin purposes. She could perhaps borrow from a bank and use the value of the cash gold as collateral.

Precious metal spreads all have this implied yield feature. It is this direct correlation with short-term interest rates which allows the trader to seek profits in carrying charge change spreads.

By knowing the current short-term interest rate and the price of the lead option in the precious metals spread, the spreader can ascertain the value of the spread. Table 6.1 is a matrix that cross-indexes the price of the lead option of a gold spread with the implied short-term interest rate. This particular matrix is for any gold spread with six months between the two options, for example, March/September or August/February. By looking where the various columns and rows cross the spread trader can ascertain the value of a gold spread.

Let's assume that the price of the December gold contract is $475 and that short-term interest rates are running around 16%. By follow-

Table 6.1 Gold Straddle Matrix

Implied Interest Rate	Gold Price									
	325	350	375	400	425	450	475	500	525	550
10	16.3	17.5	18.8	20.0	21.5	22.5	23.8	25.0	26.5	27.5
11	17.9	19.25	20.6	22.0	23.4	24.8	26.1	27.5	28.9	30.3
12	19.5	21	22.5	24.0	25.5	27.0	28.5	30.0	31.5	33.0
13	21.1	22.8	24.4	26.0	27.6	29.3	30.9	32.5	34.1	35.8
14	22.8	24.5	26.3	28.0	29.8	31.5	33.3	35.0	36.8	38.5
15	24.4	26.3	28.1	30.0	31.9	33.8	35.6	37.5	39.4	41.3
16	26	28	30.0	32.0	34.0	36.0	38.0	40.0	42.0	44.0
17	27.6	29.8	31.9	34.0	36.1	38.3	40.4	42.5	44.6	46.8
18	29.3	31.5	33.8	36.0	38.3	40.5	42.8	45.0	47.3	49.5
19	30.9	33.3	35.6	38.0	40.4	42.8	45.1	47.5	49.9	52.3
20	32.5	35	37.5	40.0	42.5	45.0	47.5	50.0	52.5	55.0

ing the $475 column down to the 16% row, it can be seen that the value of the December/June spread is $38. It is actually easier to work it another way. Look at the settlement prices of the December contract and the following June contract. The trader can see, for example, that the following June contract closed $38 higher at $513. The trader could then find the implied yield by looking down the row that the $38 fell on.

It should be obvious that a matrix similar to this one could be constructed for a greater range of prices and yields and in greater detail. Instead of price gradations of $25 per ounce from $375 to $575, the trader could construct one with $5 gradations from $100 to $1,000.

A matrix could also be constructed for different time periods and different precious metals. This one was developed for six month gold spreads. The spread aficionado could put one together for three month silver spreads or twelve month platinum spreads or whatever.

The use of the matrix in trading is simple. The trader first finds the current situation on the matrix. He then projects a future price of gold and a future short-term interest rate. He cross-indexes the two projections and arrives at an estimate of the spread value if those two conditions existed. Should the reward/risk ratio be appropriate, the trader then initiates his trade.

March gold is trading at $500 an ounce. Short-term interest rates are running 18%. The March/September gold spread is thus worth about $45. The spread trader believes that short-term rates are going to decline to 13% while the price of March Gold is going to decline to $400. By using the matrix, the spread trader is able to come up with an objective of $26 for the spread. He is thus projecting a profit of $19 per ounce, or $1,900 per contract.

The matrix can also be helpful in those situations when the price action and the interest rates are partially offsetting each other. Suppose the trader still believed that the price would drop from $500 to $400 per ounce but that short-term rates would rise from the current 18% to 20%. How much effect does the one factor offset the other? In this example, the matrix shows that at $400 and 20% the March/September gold spread would be worth about $40. The prospective gain would shrink from $1,900 to $500. The trader may still want to initiate the spread but his enthusiasm will surely be less.

   Much of the time, the spread trader will examine carrying charges to determine their effect on a spread that he wishes to put on for some other reason. Before putting on any spread in a storable commodity, the spread trader must examine the prospects for interest rates to determine the effect they will have on the carrying charges. For example, a trader may want to put on a bull spread in pork bellies and yet, at the same time, interest rates may be rising and appear as if they will continue to rise. The rise in interest rates will tend to move the spread in favor of carrying charges while the trader is looking for a move in the opposite direction. The spreader must determine the amount of change that the carrying charge will move in order to determine whether it will offset the bull move that was expected because of other analysis. This is an example of a change in carrying charges taking away what could be the potential advantages of the spread.

   On the other hand, if the trader had wanted to put on a bear spread in pork bellies and carrying charges were expected to widen, the trader would have an extra kicker in his trade.

   Carrying charges can also change simply because the absolute price of the underlying commodity changes. The spread trader must determine whether price changes will help or hurt his spread. If a spreader has a spread in silver where he sold the far contract and bought the near, and if the price of silver was rising, this would have the effect of widening the carrying charges. This could possibly eliminate the profit he was looking for. Conversely, if silver prices drop, the carrying charges would narrow.

   Because of the increasing volatility of interest rates and commodity prices, carrying charge spreads can become very profitable. Gold in 1980 and 1981 is a prime example. While the price of gold was soaring, gold spreads were having moves that were the same magnitude as the outright had had only a few months earlier. From July 1979 until February 1980, the six month gold spreads moved from approximately $15 premium the far contract to over $70 premium the far. This move of $55 represents a value of $5,500!

   Spreads in the foreign currencies represent another case where carrying charges are the main feature in the spreads. Currency spreads are largely determined by interest rate differences between the United States and the foreign country. This is true whether it be the Swiss franc, the British pound, the Japanese yen, the Canadian dollar, or the Deutschemark. The other factor affecting the foreign currency spreads is the market's expectations, which are usually reflected in the cash forward quotation market.

The Mexican peso spreads continually have the far months selling for less than the near months. This is not unusual and could be predicted by looking at the interest rate differential between the United States and Mexico. The peso spreads, however, will occasionally widen dramatically beyond their carrying charges, as rumors arise that the Mexican government is going to allow the value of the peso to drop. Speculators need the additional incentive of deferred contracts going beyond carrying charges to hold deferred contracts of pesos during such periods of uncertainty. If the devaluation does not occur, the spreads move back to the level indicated by the carrying charges.

Because the carrying charge for a currency spread is the difference between the interest rates in the two countries, the trader is speculating partially on United States interest rates and partially on foreign interest rates. As the difference between the two interest rates rises and falls, the currency spreads widen and narrow. If interest rates are higher in another country than in the United States, the far foreign currency contracts will be priced lower than the near contracts. As the difference between the United States and foreign interest rates narrows, the currency spread will narrow. Should the interest rates in the United States go above the foreign currency's, the far contracts of the foreign currency will go to premium over the near contracts.

Remember, this is the usual case. The expectations of the market can distort spread differences away from what their interest rate differential would imply. In fact, these expectations may be what the spreader is looking for. When the expectations have taken the spread away from its interest rate base, the spread trader may want to initiate a spread looking for a return to interest rate differentials.

The general rule to remember, though, is that if a country has higher interest rates than the United States, its currency will be discounted in the deferred futures market, and if the countries interest rates are lower than in the United States, the far contracts of its currency will be at a premium.

This follows good common sense. Suppose interest rates were 5% in West Germany and 15% in the United States. If the Deutschemark was selling for 50¢ in the spot cash market and 50¢ in the one year futures, the investor would simply sell his Deutschemarks and buy dollars, thus reaping an additional 10% per annum on his investment.

Many people would borrow Deutschmarks, paying the 5% interest. They would then put their money into U.S. dollars, collecting 15% interest on their deposit. They would be collecting a net 10% return with no net investment. All other things being equal, the large buying of U.S. dollars and selling of Deutschemarks will cause the U.S. dollar to gain on the Deutschemark. In the real world, the Deutschemark will gain in value in the deferred futures by the amount necessary to offset the interest rate advantage of the U.S. dollar. In this example, the Deutschemark contract one year in the future will be valued 10% higher than the spot Deutschemark. If the spot Deutschemark was at 50¢, the one year forward contract would trade around 55¢. The 10% higher price in the far contract would result from the actions of currency spreaders and arbitrageurs.

It should be noted that the model presented will not work if there are restrictions on the free flow of funds between the two countries or if market participants are expecting a change in the value of the currency. Both factors could induce some traders to override the interest rate differentials as a rationale for being in the market.

The theory that forward foreign exchange rates will move to offset changes in relative interest rates is called the interest rate parity theory. Thus if the Swiss franc, valued at 60¢, has short-term rates at 4% and the U.S. short rates are at 8%, the forward value of a three month forward contract will be 60.6¢ (8% minus 4% equals 4% times 60¢ equals 2.4¢ divided by 12 months equals .2¢ times 3 months equals .6¢ plus 60¢ equals 60.6¢). Should U.S. rates increase to 9% while the Swiss rates stay at 4%, the Swiss franc three month forward rate would adjust from the 60.6¢ to 60.75¢.

To sum up, the trader's strategy would be:

Expectation	Action
U.S. rates gain on foreign rates	Sell the near foreign currency and buy the far
U.S. rates lose to the foreign rates	Buy the near contract and sell the far

Table 6.2 Three Month Japanese Yen Spreads

Implied Interest Rate	Yen Price								
	45.00	45.50	46.00	46.50	47.00	47.50	48.00	48.50	49.00
1.00	0.11	0.11	0.12	0.12	0.12	0.12	0.12	0.12	0.12
2.00	0.23	0.23	0.23	0.24	0.24	0.24	0.24	0.24	0.25
3.00	0.34	0.34	0.35	0.35	0.35	0.36	0.36	0.36	0.37
4.00	0.45	0.46	0.46	0.47	0.47	0.48	0.48	0.49	0.49
5.00	0.56	0.57	0.58	0.58	0.59	0.59	0.60	0.61	0.61
6.00	0.68	0.68	0.69	0.70	0.71	0.71	0.72	0.73	0.74
7.00	0.79	0.80	0.81	0.81	0.82	0.83	0.84	0.85	0.86
8.00	0.90	0.91	0.92	0.93	0.94	0.95	0.96	0.97	0.98
9.00	1.01	1.02	1.04	1.05	1.06	1.07	1.08	1.09	1.10
10.00	1.13	1.14	1.15	1.16	1.18	1.19	1.20	1.21	1.23
11.00	1.24	1.25	1.27	1.28	1.29	1.31	1.32	1.33	1.35

The best way to get a handle on currency spreads is to construct a matrix similar to the one developed for gold earlier in this chapter. Table 6.2 is used the same way as the gold matrix. The only difference is that the spread could be positive or negative. In other words, the September/December Japanese yen spread could be 25 points premium the December, or, if Japanese interest rates were higher than U.S. rates, the December contract could be 25 points discounted to the September. Therefore, to use this charge, the trader must recognize which situations will cause the spread to be positive or negative. The trader should also note that the matrix is for three month yen spreads. For six month spreads, double the differences; for nine month spreads triple the differences; and so on.

This table is constructed in the same way as the gold matrix was with the exception that the interest rate differential is used instead of just borrowing costs. The interest rate differential represents the net carrying cost, which is the interest cost to borrow one currency minus the interest received in the other currency.

It can be seen that carrying charge change spreads present a tremendous opportunity to the spread trader. The key factors are the change in interest rates and the change in price level.

This type of analysis would be useful to the outright trader who is trying to select which contract to trade.

SEVEN

Bull and Bear Spreads

Bull and bear spreads are surrogate outright positions. In other words, the trader has an option of putting on an interdelivery bull or bear spread instead of an outright long or short. Since nearby contracts generally gain on distant contracts in a bull market and lose value in a bear market, a bull spread consists of being long the nearby contract and short the deferred contract. Conversely, a bear spread is long the far contract and short the near contract.

When a trader, through various types of analysis, decides that a market will be in an upward trend, he may place bull spreads instead of outright long positions. The reverse is also true. A trader, looking at a market which appears to have burdensome supplies, has the option of placing a bear spread instead of shorting the market. The most common substitute for an outright position is intercrop spreads. The trader who wishes to go long could instead buy the old crop and sell the new crop if she was looking for a near-term tightness in supplies.

There is typically much less volatility in a bull or bear spread then in an outright position. This is usually true even in the case of a new crop/old crop spread. A common example of a new crop/old crop spread being used as a surrogate for a long or short position is the July/November soybean spread. The spread has about half the volatility of an outright position but the margin typically runs only 20%

61

of outright position margins. This way the trader has much greater leverage per dollar of margin in the effort to capitalize on either a bull or bear market. This is an advantage if the spread works and the trader has a much greater return on investment. On the other hand, this trader will be wiped out five times more quickly than a trader with an outright position would have been.

It should be noted that a bull or bear spread is not always as good as an outright position. Prices can move for technical reasons rather than fundamental and the price can, for instance, go up without the bull spread working. Alternatively, the spread can move in the proper direction but the outright may not—or may even go in the opposite direction.

It should also be noted that when a trader has a bull spread on and the price of the underlying commodity rises for technical reasons, the spread may actually work in an opposite direction. Spreads frequently remain at a stable percentage of full carry. When the price of the underlying commodity rises the spread will move outward toward full carry because the actual amount of full carry has moved out. The spread will have remained at the same percentage of full carry as previously but the actual value would have changed.

The use of bull spreads as surrogate long positions is a particularly attractive proposition when they can be initiated during a carrying charge market. This limits the risk while leaving the profit potential open. The trader must be very farsighted to use this technique since it may take many months for the bullish conditions to emerge in the marketplace and provide the bull spreader with a profit.

The choice of whether a trader should utilize a bull or bear spread or simply go with the outright positions is a matter that should be determined on a trade-by-trade basis. The risk/reward ratio frequently favors one approach over the other. Also, absolute price levels may be important. Outright purchases of a commodity near historic lows may be a wiser approach than bull spreading.

Nonetheless, the mere fact of generally low risk can make them a worthwhile substitute, particularly for novices or conservative traders. The decreased volatility can provide the extra margin of psychological security that they may desire.

The novice trader can practice analyzing a particular commodity and can put on a spread instead of putting on an outright position.

The trader practices analysis but with less risk. This can substantially cut down the losses that the novice trader is usually burdened with while learning methods of commodity analysis.

The most important thing for the bull and bear spreader to do is analyze the underlying commodity. This can be any type of analysis—technical, seasonal, or fundamental. The preferred method, however, is fundamental, because bull and bear spreads typically respond to the fundamentals in a commodity rather than the technicals. Though this is not always the case, the trader will gain by concentrating on the fundamentals rather than the technicals. We saw that a spread can actually go the wrong way if the trader initiates it only on technical grounds. This happens frequently enough so that it must be mentioned. The advantage of fundamental analysis is that it tries to ascertain whether or not a commodity is in a potentially tight supply/demand situation. This is precisely the type of situation that a bull or bear spread is concerned with.

There are some commodities that bull and bear spreads work on and there are commodities where the reverse is true or where there is no relationship. Bull and bear spreads work on commodities where, in fundamentally oriented bull markets, the nears gain on the fars. In technically oriented markets, even spreads in the commodities listed below will not necessarily follow the general pattern. Commodities in which the usual pattern applies include:

Cocoa	Pork bellies
Copper	Soybeans
Corn	Soybean meal
Cotton	Soybean oil
Oats	Sugar
Orange juice	Wheat
Plywood	

The commodities which work in the opposite direction include:

Gold	Potatoes
Platinum	Silver

What would be called a bear spread in most commodities would be a bull spread in these commodities. In other words, the trader would put on a short nearby/long deferred spread if he anticipated higher prices in the underlying commodity. This is the exact reverse of the general pattern of most commodities. These commodities tend to be in a pattern of the far contracts always being higher than the nears.

Bull markets in the precious metals, gold, silver, and platinum occur because of a change in the market's evaluation of the commodity. Bull markets do not occur in precious metals because of a tightness of supplies. There are huge worldwide stocks of each of these commodities, which, though not necessarily in deliverable positions, can be quickly pulled into deliverable positions. Thus what might be a burdensome supply in other commodities keeps the value of the spreads at or very near full carry. When the price of the commodity goes up, the amount of full carry widens and the far contracts gain on the near. The precious metals are thus more on the order of a carrying charge change spread than anything else.

The precious metals will act like the majority of commodities in rare instances only. There have been occasions when there has been a threat of market participants taking delivery of all of the silver in deliverable stocks. This has had the effect of forcing the expiring contract to move to a premium over the next contract available. From that point on, however, the premium of the far months over the nears has been the usual pattern in precious metals.

Potatoes, on the other hand, do not conform to the general pattern because they have a high degree of perishability and a seasonal production cycle. The round white potatoe contract, traded on the New York Mercantile Exchange, calls for delivery of potatoes grown in New York, Connecticut, and Maine and harvested in the fall. November is considered the first new crop futures contract for the potato contract. The potatoes are placed in storage in November and are consumed throughout the winter, but the supplies are usually used up by June of the following year. Until recently, there had been a May contract which was considered the last futures in the crop year. Since the Commodity Futures Trading Commission banned May potato contracts, however, the April contract has now become potentially tight. Thus the April contract will always be at a premium to the November contract. If something is going to be bullish for the November contract, it is going to be even more bullish for the April contract.

The far contract also commands a premium because the market must compensate the holder of the potatoes for the loss of opportunities to use the money invested in the potatoes, lost interest on the money invested in the potatoes, and the risks due to the high perishability of the potatoes. This is a further incentive for the far months to be at a premium to the near months. For instance, should many of the potatoes still be in the fields in the middle of the winter and a freeze-thaw–freeze-thaw cycle occur, the potatoes will be severely damaged. Thus the risks of further damage are greater for the April contract than for the February contract even though the cycle may have occurred in January. The greater amount of time increases the chances of something going wrong.

The spread trader should note that the spread between one crop year and the next crop year, for example, April 1981 versus November 1981, should be treated as an intercommodity spread even though potatoes are being traded. This is because the supply and demand fundamentals are completely different between the two crop years. Potatoes from one crop year will not last long enough, due to their perishability, to be delivered into the following crop year.

Nonstorable commodities (cattle, feeder cattle, live hogs, and—should they ever become more popular—broilers and eggs) are commodities that tend to have no relationship between the outright price movement and the movement of the spreads, because it is virtually impossible to deliver such a commodity from one delivery period to another. In other words, the trader who took delivery of live cattle in June would be extremely unlikely to redeliver them against the August contract. Each contract month is considered as a separate commodity.

Because the marketplace views each separate contract month as a separate commodity, it is not unusual to see a U.S. Department of Agriculture report result in prices of different contract months moving in opposite directions. For example, if the March Hogs and Pigs Report showed that there was a very large supply of hogs weighing over 180 pounds, ready to come to market, the April live hog contract would be depressed. If the report also showed that hogs under 60 pounds that would be ready for delivery in several months were down dramatically from the previous year, the October contract would rally sharply. Once again, it can be seen that each contract must be considered as a separate commodity. This makes the spreads particularly treacherous when major government reports such as the Hogs and Pigs Report and the quarterly Cattle on Feed Report are issued. We can sum up by saying that nonstorable commodity spreads reflect the varying perceptions of the relative supply and demand between the different contracts.

It must be remembered, particularly in conjunction with these types of nonstorable commodity spreads, that the market tends to discount what is known. In other words, after a major report comes out, the market will react swiftly to reflect the new supply/demand situation. It is up to the analyst in these commodities to come to a conclusion different from the market. This could be done by a superior interpretation of the facts outlined in the report or it could be done by examining the actual slaughter figures during the period after the report. For instance, the report might show that hog slaughter will be 100% of the previous year's hog slaughter for the next month, but the actual slaughter may come out to be 105% of the previous year's slaughter. If the analyst felt that this condition would continue to occur, he would have the opportunity to sell the nearby contract and buy the far, all other things being equal. Once again, this type of analysis will be unsuitable if the market has also reacted to the same actual slaughter figures.

There can be, for a short time only, an extra push on the near contract due to the greater speculative interest in the nearby contract. Speculators tend to speculate in the lead month. Speculators will trade July soybeans during June. In a bull market, the extra buying power of the speculators can often push the July contract up a bit over what the commercial interests might expect to see. Many times the commercial interests or spread traders will sell the nearby, in this instance, and buy the far and bring the relationships back in line. Nonetheless, speculators can push the spreads out of line over a short period of time.

An important consideration for the bull and bear spreader is the historical evidence of what the spread did during similar times in the past. In other words, given a particular supply/demand balance, was there a period in the past that was analogous? If so, what did this particular spread do in that circumstance? This type of analysis will be discussed in greater detail in Chapter 8 but it should be noted here that this is a particularly powerful tool when examining spreads for their applicability as bull or bear spreads.

There are several exceptions to the general patterns that work in favor of the spreader. First, technical action may push the spread in the direction that does not reflect the underlying fundamentals. It is not uncommon to see soybeans rally 15¢ on floor trader short covering and then start to trigger buy stops. This can have the effect of moving the price up 50¢ and doing nothing for the spreads. This, however, has the important side-effect of alerting the trader to the fact that the rally is a technical rally rather than a fundamentally based rally. This can alert traders to good short sell opportunities. Also, the reverse is true. The market can drop on long liquidation without the spreads moving toward full carry. This is also an alert for the astute trader that the bear move was probably a result of speculative technical actions rather than commercial fundamental action.

Second, when a market has moved from a carrying charge market to an inverted market, the premiums that the nearby contracts command over the far contracts may become so large that the fundamentals cannot support a further rise. This is the most dangerous point to put on a bull spread. When the premiums have already moved from a carrying charge market to an inverted market, the marketplace has probably already discounted, or certainly is in the process of discounting, the obviously bullish fundamentals. The underlying price of the commodity can continue to move up, although most likely for a short time, and yet the spread may level out or even begin to move in a bear direction.

Third, spreads that have as one leg the expiring month frequently move in the direction contrary to what one might expect. This is particularly applicable after the first notice day for a commodity. A contract during the delivery month will often move due to what might be considered very short-term technical considerations such as the position of deliverable stocks and the stock requirements of commercial interests. The first consideration, deliverable stocks, is a known quantity, published weekly over the major wire services, and this information can be obtained through a broker. Unfortunately, the second point, the needs and wants of the large commercial interests, are known only to themselves. The trader can gain insight into these needs and wants by the initial period of deliveries and redeliveries, but this is of little use to the majority of spread traders. By the time the trader had determined whether the commercials want or desire to take delivery or make delivery, the spreader is usually in the position of having to make or take delivery. The extra costs and inconveniences make this a dubious time to be initiating spreads.

Fourth, government actions can also play a role in determing spread relationships. The price controls put on by Richard Nixon did much to distort normal spread relationships. The grain embargo initiated by Jimmy Carter also had a profound influence. Grains in government reserve programs have had an effect on spread relationships.

Let's look a little closer at the reserve. The amount of grain on the free market generally is substantially less than the total of all of the available stocks. It is not uncommon to see the carryout of corn appear to be 1 billion bushels, with only 100 million of that billion bushels in the so-called free market. This means that prices have not risen to the point necessary for the government to release the stocks in the reserve or loan program, so there is no direct effect on spread relationships.

It should be clear that bull and bear spreads contain significant potential for profit, but they are a more complicated subject than the very simplistic carrying charge spreads that we had been examining.

EIGHT

Historical Comparison Analysis

Historical comparison analysis consists of finding periods in the past that are similar to the current fundamental situation and applying data from earlier spread price action to the current scene. The assumption is that similar conditions will produce similar price behavior.

Spreads initiated without regard to historical patterns are shots in the dark. There are many instances when the fundamentals of a commodity will look very bullish or bearish, yet the price will move opposite to what was indicated by the fundamentals. The futures market often discounts the effect of future fundamentals in today's price. The market's expectations can move the price levels far beyond what current fundamentals dictate. When the fundamental situation that the market was discounting finally occurs the price often moves in the opposite direction.

At other times, the market will move very closely in step with the current fundamentals. Historical comparison analysis can help reveal the character of the market. It allows the analyst to gain insights into how the market will react to a given fundamental situation. In this regard it is similar to technical analysis. One theory behind technical

69

analysis is that, given a particular price pattern, subsequent prices will be similar to what happened after prior occurrences of the same pattern. The theory behind historical comparison analysis is that price patterns will be similar given similar fundamental conditions or patterns.

An excellent example of a price move opposite to the apparent fundamentals occurred in 1976/77. Cotton prices rallied sharply in the early part of that crop year. In fact, much of the upward price movement occurred before the crop year began. There were expectations of a small cotton crop. These expectations, which became fact, moved prices higher as the market discounted a potentially tight supply/demand situation. The tight supply/demand situation became a reality but the price movement before the crop year began effectively discounted the known or expected fundamentals.

The same situation happened with interdelivery cotton spreads. The market had expected the tight supply/demand condition even before the crop year began. The March 1977 contract moved to over 600 points above the July 1977 contract in June 1976. This spread differential more than compensated for the predicted reduction of carryover stocks. Even with the reduction of stocks, there was a sufficient amount of cotton to meet the demand. The price of the spread collapsed so much that in January 1977, the March contract was more than 100 points under the July contract. The spread had moved over 750 points. Even though the fundamentals were bullish during the actual 1976/77 crop year, the supply/demand tightness had already been discounted. As the expectation of the crop year became a reality, the bullishness was replaced by a new reality.

If prices discount the future, as they did in this example, the discounted price becomes a factor which tends to offset itself. This probably sounds confusing but really is quite simple. If the supply of cotton looks like it will be down in the coming crop year, the price of cotton will move up because of an expected tightness in the supply/demand situation. The new higher price, however, will cause buyers of the commodity to reduce their demand. The demand will usually be reduced to a level that the supply will be adequate for.

It can be seen that there are many similarities between the historical comparison method and the methods outlined in bull and bear analysis. Both seek to examine the fundamentals of a market to give an insight into future price behavior. The major difference is that the historical comparison method finds prior years with similar fundamental characteristics from which the trader can gain additional insight into future price behavior.

How quickly could the spread trader of 1981 have utilized historical comparison analysis for trading cotton spreads? Let's suppose that the trader, perhaps because of other forms of spread analysis or perhaps because of a hunch that there will be a lot of action, looks at the October/December cotton spread.

The spread trader should develop a series of ratios to help determine which past years are similar to the current situation. The ratios must be selected on the basis of applicability. For instance, the spread we are examining, October/December cotton, is a new crop/old crop spread. Thus we would be interested primarily in ratios of fundamental factors which zero in on the old crop versus new crop fundamentals. After selecting the ratios that are expected to illustrate the current situation, the trader should use correlation analysis, as described in Chapter 10, to determine how much correlation there is between movements in the ratios and movements in the spread price. We might look at the following ratios as being indicative of new crop versus old crop supply and demand:

1. Ending stocks divided by new crop production. This ratio is a very clear indicator of old crop demand, as shown in ending stocks, versus new crop production, which is a proxy for new crop supply.
2. Production divided by previous year's production. The production of each year gives us an indication of the relative supplies for the two different years.
3. Ending stocks versus demand. Both of these numbers come from the old crop and both show an indication of the old crop's supply and demand situation. This is necessary because the old crop tends to have an important effect on this spread.
4. Demand versus supply. This is the total demand for a commodity divided by the total supply for the commodity. This ratio is much the same as the previous ratio. The nearby contract, October, tends to have a greater influence on the spread than does the

December contract. It is for this reason that we examine closely
the old crop fundamentals.

5. Demand versus new crop production. This is the total demand
for one crop year versus the production for the coming crop year.
This is another indicator of the old crop fundamental situation in
relation to the new crop fundamental situation.

All of these ratios have a high degree of correlation with the price of
the October/December cotton spread. Some ratios without a high
degree of correlation include exports versus ending stocks and ending
stocks versus the previous year's ending stocks.

Because it is a new crop/old crop spread, the ratios tend to zero in
on new crop/old crop conditions, with less emphasis on old crop
conditions. The trader examining a spread that was within one market
and within one crop year should examine more closely ratios such as
demand over supply, which give indications of prices within the same
crop year.

Table 8.1 gives the basic supply and demand information for the
1970s. This information is easily obtainable and provides virtually
everything that is needed for basic historical comparison analysis.
After the trader becomes comfortable using this basic information,
she can move into more detailed information. The trader could look
into information such as exports over a particular four-week period,
cash sales over a particular period, and basis movements over a particular time period. This additional information will give the trader
more grist for the mill and thus more confidence in trading.

Although the construction of the ratios is simple, it is important
not to be confused by the seasonal year designations. When we speak
of the ending stocks/new crop production ratio we are talking about
the ending stocks of the current crop year versus the production of
the new crop year. In June 1980 the ending stocks would be of the
1980/81 season and the new crop production would be of the 1981/82
crop year. Table 8.2 shows the aforementioned five ratios for 1971 to
1980.

The next task facing the historical comparison analyst is to determine which years were the closest to the current situation. This way,
the trader will know which years may provide useful guidelines. After
constructing the ratios for past years the trader must construct the

Table 8.1   Cotton: Supply and Disappearance, by Type, United States

	Supply				Disappearance				
Year Beginning August 1	Beginning Stocks, August 1	Pro- duction	Imports	Total	Mill Con- sumption	Exports	Total	Difference Unac- counted	Ending Stocks, July 31
				1,000 480-Pound Net Weight Bales					
				All Kinds					
1971	4,203	10,477	72	14,752	8,259	3,385	11,644	150	3,258
1972	3,258	13,704	34	16,996	7,769	5,311	13,080	305	4,221
1973	4,221	12,974	48	17,243	7,472	6,123	13,595	160	3,808
1974	3,808	11,540	34	15,382	5,860	3,926	9,786	112	5,708
1975	5,708	8,302	92	14,102	7,250	3,311	10,561	140	3,681
1976	3,681	10,581	38	14,300	6,674	4,784	11,458	86	2,928
1977	2,928	14,389	5	17,322	6,483	5,484	11,967	−8	5,347
1978	5,347	10,856	4	16,207	6,352	6,180	12,532	283	3,958
1979	3,958	14,629	5	18,592	6,506	9,229	15,735	142	3,000
1980	3,000	11,122	28	14,150	5,891	5,926	11,817	335	2,668

Source: U.S. Department of Agriculture, 1981.

Table 8.2 Cotton Fundamental Ratios

	(1) Ending Stocks/ New Crop Production	(2) New Crop Production/ Previous Year's Production	(3) Ending Stocks/ Demand	(4) Demand/ Supply	(5) Demand/ New Crop Production
1971	.24	1.31	.28	.79	.85
1972	.33	.95	.32	.77	1.01
1973	.33	.89	.28	.79	1.05
1974	.69	.72	.58	.64	1.18
1975	.35	1.27	.35	.75	1.00
1976	.20	1.36	.26	.80	.80
1977	.49	.75	.45	.69	1.10
1978	.27	1.37	.32	.77	.84
1979	.27	.76	.19	.83	1.38
1980	.20	.74	.24	.81	.83

Table 8.3   U.S. Supply/Demand for Cotton (July 13, 1981)

	1980/81	1981/82
Supply		
Beginning stocks	3.0	2.5
Production	11.1	13.8
Total supply	14.2	16.3
Disappearance		
Mill use	5.8	6.1
Exports	6.0	6.7
Total use	11.8	12.8
Unaccounted	0.1	.1
Ending stocks	2.5	3.6

expected ratios for the current year. The trader can use the U.S. Department of Agriculture supply/demand estimates or can construct an original chart. For simplicity's sake, let's assume that the trader uses the USDA figures. Table 8.3 presents the supply and demand estimates for 1980/81 and 1981/82 which were released on July 13, 1981. It should be noted that these estimates were not particularly accurate but they are the estimates that the market was working with. The trader should then construct the same ratios using the current year's data. In our example, ratio 1, ending stocks versus new crop production would equal .17. Ratio 2, production versus previous years production, would equal 1.24. Ratio 3, ending stocks versus demand, would equal .20. Ratio 4, demand versus supply, would equal .81. Ratio 5, demand versus next year's production, would equal .86.

The next step is to scan the table of previous years to find the years that were closest to the ratios of this year. Table 8.4 summarizes

Table 8.4   Comparison Yearly Chart

	Ratio				
	1	2	3	4	5
Years Closest to	1976	1975	1980	1980	1978
Current Year	1980	1971	1976	1976	1971

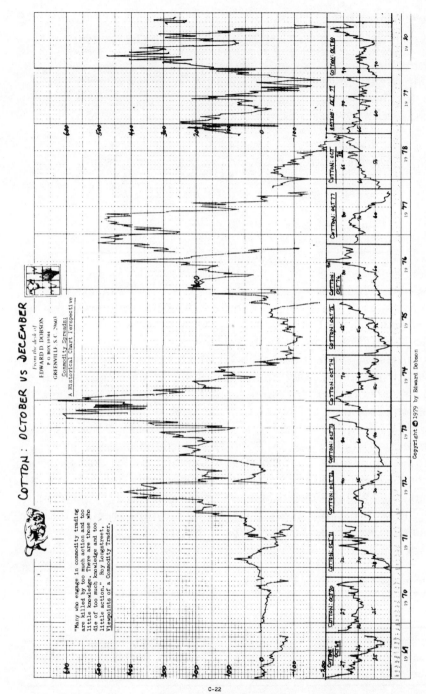

Figure 8.1 October/December cotton spread history.

the results of finding the two years closest to the current year's situation. It can be easily seen that 1976 and 1980 were the two years most closely related to the current year's fundamentals, but 1971 should also get an honorable mention. Thus the spread trader will examine the price in 1976 and 1980 with a lesser emphasis on the behavior in 1971.

Figure 8.1 shows the price behavior of the October versus December cotton spread from 1969 to 1980. The trader should zero in on the three years just selected as being the most representative. She should further take a look at only the time period that she is going to be trading, July 1 through October 1. It can be seen that in all three years the October contract lost significantly to the December contract. In 1971 the spread lost only about 50 points, but in 1976 there was a loss of several hundred points and the same situation occurred in 1980. The trader would conclude that she would want to put on a bear spread by buying December 1980 and selling October 1980 cotton.

Figure 8.2 shows what actually happened after June 30. The price broke down below support at about 130 premium October, fell significantly, and hit a low of about −175. Thus the expected price behavior occured. The astute trader, after examining the historical evidence, would have been in a position to profit handsomely in this trade. By combining historical comparison analysis with other techniques the

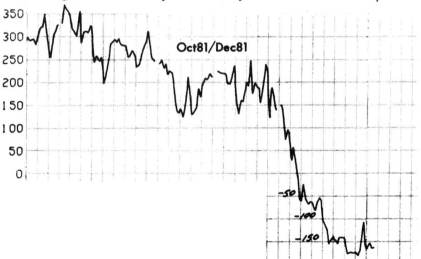

Figure 8.2   October 1981/December 1981 cotton spread.

trader may be in a position to find additional profit-making trades.

The use of historical comparison can also pinpoint what has happened in previous periods of major trends of the underlying commodity. The trader who is examining a particular bull or bear spread can gain insight into the relative risk and reward of a trade. If the price of July soybeans moves $1.00, what has been the effect on the July/November soybean spread in the past? Figure 8.3 gives an example of price behavior of the July contract across the bottom with the July/November spread across the top. The trader can then see how the price of the July contract affects the spread. He might combine this with the ratio analysis outlined above. If he has an opinion on where the outright July price would go, he will also get an idea of where the July/November spread might go. Examination of past behavior should provide some idea of the magnitude of the spread price move based on an estimate of the move in the July contract. If, for instance, the trader thought that conditions were similar to early 1972, he would examine the 1972 charts to estimate the magnitude of the move. In this case, the price of soybeans moved from about $3.20 a bushel to $3.60 a bushel for a net move of about 40¢. During the same time, the July/November spread moved about 20¢. In other words, for every 1-¢ move in the July contract, the July/November spread moved ½¢. If in the current year the trader felt that the July contract was going to move up $1.00 and gain on the November, he could estimate that the July would gain about 50¢ on the November contract. This process gives the bull and bear spreader an idea of what conditions need to occur to make his bull or bear spread a successful one.

The trader can also see what happens to spread price levels in a particular commodity when the markets were supply/demand or spec-

Although spreads can deviate from historical patterns, the trader can usually assign upper or lower boundaries on the expected current price behavior. This is an enormous help in ascertaining the risk that is necessary to put on a trade as well as the potential reward. Any movement into new historical areas is, by definition, an extraordinary event. Because it is always better to bet against extraordinary events, the trader would be increasing the odds by bear spreading close to the previous extreme. On the reward side, the trader can ascertain the expected limits of a move. If he wanted to buy December corn and sell July corn at 15¢ premium the December corn, and he knew that it

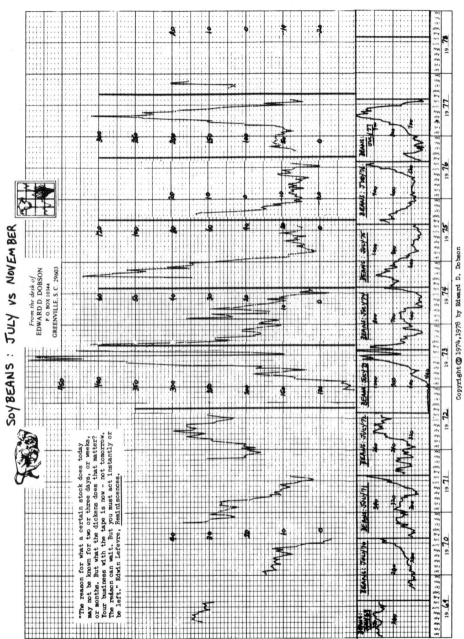

Figure 8.3 July/November soybean spread history.

had never gone over 25¢ premium December, the trader could expect that his profit would be limited to 10¢ or less.

The use of historical spread analysis can be considered as a largely defensive strategy. It will show the trader the potential risk and reward of a trade as well as keeping the trader out of trades that go against historical evidence. For example, given a particular supply/demand situation, if a spread has moved away from full carrying charges from January to March for each of the last ten years, the trader should take a second look at doing any bear spreading during that time period. He would have to have some extraordinarily bearish news to motivate him to go against that kind of historical evidence. This historical perspective will stop the trader from making some trades because he will see that a move into new historical ground is needed to profit from a given trade. The defensive aspect of historical analysis is one of its most valuable attributes.

Some traders may scoff at the desirability of defensive examination of historical levels. However, experience has shown that when prices move to new historical levels, they often overshoot the previous level by a significant amount. The price of nearly all commodities moved dramatically beyond their previous highs during 1973 and 1974.

Historical comparison analysis can be used to suggest new trades, to ascertain risk/reward ratios, and to provide a useful adjunct to other techniques, especially bull and bear spreading.

NINE

Seasonal Analysis

One of the most powerful techniques for analyzing spreads is seasonal analysis. It can be used as a technique for obtaining spread ideas as well as analyzing spreads that were considered for other reasons.

Seasonal price fluctuations are the cyclical fluctuations in the price of a spread during the year. A seasonal spread is a spread which tends to have a particular price movement during a particular time of the year. As with all commodities and commodity investments, some spreads have a seasonal pattern while others have little or none. Moreover, sometimes the reason for a seasonal pattern can be ascertained and at other times the spread will exhibit seasonality for no reason that the analyst can discover. This may result from ignorance on the part of the analyst who has not delved deeply enough into the subject. Nonetheless, a high reliability of seasonality can be adequate justification for a trade.

One of the major uses of seasonality is as a defensive tactic. Often a trader will wish to initiate a particular spread for other reasons. Perhaps the trader is looking at some bull or bear spread or at some kind of carrying charge situation. No matter what the mode of analysis, the spread trader should always examine the seasonality of a spread. It is not uncommon for a trader to want to initiate a particular spread only to find out that there are seasonal pressures working against the trade. On the other hand, the trader may find additional ammunition for initiating a particular spread. The defensive aspect centers around the persuasive power of a strong seasonality working against the trader's proposed trade. The trader who wants to bear spread December 1981 versus May 1982 wheat in the middle of November had better have strong reasons for doing so, because December gains on May 90% of the time during the month of November. If the seasonality is only 50%, the analyst can easily ignore it. The main justification in examining seasonality is as an effort to get the odds in the trader's favor. When one can trade knowing that nine out of ten times a trade will be favorable, the trader has much more confidence, peace of mind, and profit. Trading commodity spreads without an examination of seasonality is like betting on the horse races without knowing the odds.

Seasonal tendencies occur in the real world because of the periodicity of events. The yearly cycle of harvesting is a classic example of seasonality in spreads. Virtually all grains have their spreads closest to full carrying charges during the harvest period. This is the time when supply is the greatest and spreads must widen to encourage the carrying of the commodity. After harvesting their wheat, for example, farmers must sell much of it to make room for the rest of the crop and to raise the cash necessary to pay off loans acquired during the planting and growing seasons. The supply of wheat may greatly exceed the demand, and the spreads widen to compensate for this greater supply. As the crop year progresses, the supply of wheat dwindles. Farmers have less need for cash and become tighter holders of their stocks; thus spreads should narrow to encourage consumption rather than storage of wheat. This pattern of widening spreads going into harvest and narrowing spreads coming out of harvest is a normal seasonal pattern in all of the grain markets. It can also be seen in any commodity that is harvested at a particular time during the year.

There are many ways to construct seasonal indexes. We will examine here two methods of discovering and quantifying seasonality. The first method is easy to construct but inaccurate. The second method gains greatly in accuracy but also requires vastly more time to construct. In fact, the reader may prefer to use a computer or programmable calculator to construct the seasonal indexes for the second method.

Suppose a spread trader wishes to initiate a hog spread using a forecasting equation as described in Chapter 10. He would need to know what pork production will be for the coming months, so he would like to find out what the seasonality is for pork production. Suppose further that the trader has very little time to come up with a seasonal index for pork production. He would therefore use the first method—the simple average method.

Table 9.1 shows pork production on a monthly basis for the years 1971 to 1980. The first step to obtain a seasonal index based on averages is to total each of the columns. Thus the trader will be finding the total pork production in the month of January, February, and so on. This should also be done for the yearly total. Table 9.2 shows the total added to the bottom of Table 9.1.

The next step is to find the average pork production for each month by simply dividing the total pork production in a given month by the number of years. For example, the total pork production for January in the ten years under consideration was 11,763,000,000 pounds. Because we are examining ten years, the analyst merely divides 11,763,000,000 by 10. This in effect moves the decimal place one position to the left. Therefore, the average January pork production for the years 1971 to 1980 was 1,176.3 million pounds. Table 9.2 has been modified and has had the average pork production per month added to it. Table 9.3 shows the new figures including the yearly total average.

The next step is to take the yearly average, 13,871.2, and divide by 12 to find the average monthly pork production: 13,871.2 divided by 12 is 1,155.9.

The final step is to derive a seasonal index by dividing the average monthly pork production by the average monthly pork production for the whole year. Thus the January average 1,176.3 is divided by the average monthly of the year 1,155.9 to yield a seasonal index of 101.8. Notice that the index number is actually multiplied by 100 to derive the index.

This procedure is followed for each of the twelve months. The yearly total, therefore, must be 1,200.0, the sum of each of the monthly seasonal indexes. Table 9.4 is the total chart, including the seasonal indexes.

The technique just outlined has some significant advantages. It is simple and relatively fast. A calculator and pen and pencil are all that is required to find the indices quickly and efficiently. Thus this system is an adequate solution for those who need a fast answer.

The method does have several drawbacks. What it gains in speed it loses in precision. Each entry that is averaged should have equal weighting. But, as can be seen in Table 9.4, there is a high degree of

Table 9.1   Red Meat Production [under federal inspection, U.S. (in millions of pounds)]

Number Pork (carcass weight)

Year	January	February	March	April	May	June	July	August	September	October	November	December	Total
1971	1,382	1,157	1,491	1,420	1,300	1,324	1,157	1,260	1,350	1,319	1,418	1,411	15,989
1972	1,182	1,143	1,436	1,242	1,271	1,193	981	1,192	1,165	1,303	1,325	1,160	14,594
1973	1,232	1,050	1,227	1,110	1,250	1,086	953	1,040	994	1,243	1,226	1,126	13,535
1974	1,293	1,060	1,255	1,315	1,370	1,143	1,100	1,202	1,226	1,326	1,214	1,164	14,668
1975	1,187	1,018	1,049	1,172	1,001	941	864	845	963	1,002	977	1,058	12,077
1976	1,024	903	1,174	1,080	951	964	914	1,102	1,167	1,285	1,347	1,220	13,132
1977	977	968	1,206	1,077	1,003	980	835	1,033	1,000	1,107	1,189	1,053	12,518
1978	1,006	972	1,135	1,053	1,033	1,007	926	1,060	1,057	1,133	1,185	1,072	12,689
1979	1,094	958	1,203	1,191	1,262	1,168	1,176	1,302	1,159	1,492	1,403	1,260	14,668
1980	1,386	1,234	1,330	1,447	1,411	1,257	1,181	1,142	1,285	1,429	1,281	1,358	15,742

Table 9.2   Red Meat Production [under federal inspection, U.S. (in millions of pounds)]

Number Pork (carcass weight)

Year	January	February	March	April	May	June	July	August	September	October	November	December	Total
1971	1,382	1,157	1,491	1,420	1,300	1,324	1,157	1,260	1,350	1,319	1,418	1,411	15,989
1972	1,182	1,143	1,436	1,242	1,271	1,193	981	1,192	1,165	1,303	1,325	1,160	14,594
1973	1,232	1,050	1,227	1,110	1,250	1,086	953	1,040	994	1,243	1,226	1,126	13,535
1974	1,293	1,060	1,255	1,315	1,370	1,143	1,100	1,202	1,226	1,326	1,214	1,164	14,668
1975	1,187	1,018	1,049	1,172	1,001	941	864	845	963	1,002	977	1,058	12,077
1976	1,024	903	1,174	1,080	951	964	914	1,102	1,167	1,285	1,347	1,220	13,132
1977	977	968	1,206	1,077	1,003	980	835	1,033	1,000	1,107	1,189	1,053	12,518
1978	1,006	972	1,135	1,053	1,033	1,007	926	1,060	1,057	1,133	1,185	1,072	12,689
1979	1,094	958	1,203	1,191	1,262	1,168	1,176	1,302	1,159	1,492	1,403	1,260	14,668
1980	1,386	1,234	1,330	1,447	1,411	1,257	1,181	1,142	1,285	1,429	1,281	1,358	15,742
Total	11,763	10,463	12,506	12,107	11,002	11,063	10,087	11,178	11,456	12,639	12,565	11,882	138,712

Table 9.3   Red Meat Production [under federal inspection, U.S. (in millions of pounds)]

Number Pork (carcass weight)

Year	January	February	March	April	May	June	July	August	September	October	November	December	Total
1971	1,382	1,157	1,491	1,420	1,300	1,324	1,157	1,260	1,350	1,319	1,418	1,411	15,989
1972	1,182	1,143	1,436	1,242	1,271	1,193	981	1,192	1,165	1,303	1,325	1,160	14,594
1973	1,232	1,050	1,227	1,110	1,250	1,086	953	1,040	994	1,243	1,226	1,126	13,535
1974	1,293	1,060	1,255	1,315	1,370	1,143	1,100	1,202	1,226	1,326	1,214	1,164	14,668
1975	1,187	1,018	1,049	1,172	1,001	941	864	845	963	1,002	977	1,058	12,077
1976	1,024	903	1,174	1,080	951	964	914	1,102	1,167	1,285	1,347	1,220	13,132
1977	977	968	1,206	1,077	1,003	980	835	1,033	1,090	1,107	1,189	1,053	12,518
1978	1,006	972	1,135	1,053	1,083	1,007	926	1,060	1,057	1,133	1,185	1,072	12,689
1979	1,094	958	1,203	1,191	1,262	1,168	1,176	1,302	1,159	1,492	1,403	1,260	14,668
1980	1,386	1,234	1,330	1,447	1,411	1,257	1,181	1,142	1,285	1,429	1,281	1,358	15,742
Total	11,763	10,463	12,506	12,107	11,902	11,063	10,087	11,178	11,456	12,639	12,565	11,882	138,712
Average	1,176.3	1,046.3	1,250.6	1,210.7	1,190.2	1,106.3	1,008.7	1,117.8	1,145.6	1,263.9	1,256.5	1,188.2	13,871.2

Table 9.4 Red Meat Production [under federal inspection, U.S. (in millions of pounds)]

Number Pork (carcass weight)

Year	January	February	March	April	May	June	July	August	September	October	November	December	Total
1971	1,382	1,157	1,491	1,420	1,300	1,324	1,157	1,260	1,350	1,319	1,418	1,411	15,989
1972	1,182	1,143	1,436	1,242	1,271	1,193	981	1,192	1,165	1,303	1,325	1,160	14,594
1973	1,232	1,050	1,227	1,110	1,250	1,086	953	1,040	994	1,243	1,226	1,126	13,535
1974	1,293	1,060	1,255	1,315	1,370	1,143	1,100	1,202	1,226	1,326	1,214	1,164	14,668
1975	1,187	1,018	1,049	1,172	1,001	941	864	845	963	1,002	977	1,058	12,077
1976	1,024	903	1,174	1,080	951	964	914	1,102	1,167	1,285	1,347	1,220	13,132
1977	977	968	1,206	1,077	1,003	980	835	1,033	1,090	1,107	1,189	1,053	12,518
1978	1,006	972	1,135	1,053	1,083	1,007	926	1,060	1,057	1,133	1,185	1,072	12,689
1979	1,094	958	1,203	1,191	1,262	1,168	1,176	1,302	1,159	1,492	1,403	1,260	14,668
1980	1,386	1,234	1,330	1,447	1,411	1,257	1,181	1,142	1,285	1,429	1,281	1,358	15,742
Total	11,763	10,463	12,506	12,107	11,902	11,063	10,087	11,178	11,456	12,639	12,565	11,882	138,712
Average	1,176.3	1,046.3	1,250.6	1,210.7	1,190.2	1,106.3	1,008.7	1,117.8	1,145.6	1,263.9	1,256.5	1,188.2	13,871.2
Index	101.8	90.5	108.2	104.7	103.0	95.7	87.3	96.7	99.1	109.3	108.7	102.8	1,200.0

fluctuation between the various months. The pork production in the month of July, for example, ranges from 835 million pounds to 1,181 million pounds. Each of these entries has equal weighting in the averaging method. When there is a very unusual number, it has the effect of moving the average away from what might be considered a more typical value. One unusual value can push the seasonal index slightly out of whack.

This problem can be solved by using the ratio to moving average method. The ratio to moving average method is much more time-consuming but the result is better than the quick approximation of the seasonal index that is provided by the average method just discussed. Let's construct a seasonal index using the same pork production figures seen in Table 9.1. Table 9.5 presents all information

Table 9.5   Pork Production—Seasonal Index Information

	(1) Pork Production	(2) Twelve-Month Moving Total	(3) Twelve-Month Moving Average: col. (2)/12	(4) Centered Twelve-Month Moving Average	(5) Specific Seasonal Indexes
1971 Jan	1,382				
Feb	1,157				
Mar	1,491				
Apr	1,420				
May	1,300				
Jun	1,324				
		15,989	1,332		
Jul	1,157			1,324	87.4
		15,789	1,316		
Aug	1,260			1,316	95.7
		15,775	1,315		
Sep	1,350			1.313	102.8
		15,720	1,310		
Oct	1,319			1,303	101.2
		15,542	1,295		
Nov	1,418			1,294	109.6
		15,513	1,293		
Dec	1,411			1,289	109.5
		15,382	1,282		

Table 9.5 (*continued*)

	(1) Pork Production	(2) Twelve-Month Moving Total	(3) Twelve-Month Moving Average: col. (2)/12	(4) Centered Twelve-Month Moving Average	(5) Specific Seasonal Indexes
1972 Jan	1,182			1,275	92.7
		15,206	1,267		
Feb	1,143			1,265	90.4
		15,138	1,262		
Mar	1,436			1,254	114.5
		14,953	1,246		
Apr	1,242			1,246	99.7
		14,937	1,245		
May	1,271			1,241	102.4
		14,844	1,237		
Jun	1,193			1,227	97.2
		14,593	1,216		
Jul	981			1,218	80.5
		14,643	1,220		
Aug	1,192			1,217	97.9
		14,550	1,213		
Sep	1,165			1,204	96.8
		14,341	1,195		
Oct	1,303			1,190	109.5
		14,209	1,184		
Nov	1,325			1,183	112.0
		14,188	1,182		
Dec	1,160			1,178	98.5
		14,081	1,173		
1973 Jan	1,232			1,172	105.1
		14,053	1,171		
Feb	1,050			1,165	90.1
		13,901	1,158		
Mar	1,227			1,151	106.6
		13,730	1,144		
Apr	1,110			1,142	97.2
		13,670	1,139		
May	1,250			1,135	110.1
		13,571	1,131		

Table 9.5 (*continued*)

		(1) Pork Production	(2) Twelve-Month Moving Total	(3) Twelve- Month Moving Average: col. (2)/12	(4) Centered Twelve- Month Moving Average	(5) Specific Season- al In- dexes
	Jun	1,086			1,130	96.3
			13,537	1,128		
	Jul	953			1,131	84.3
			13,598	1,133		
	Aug	1,040			1,134	91.7
			13,608	1,134		
	Sep	994			1,135	87.6
			13,636	1,136		
	Oct	1,243			1,145	108.6
			13,841	1,153		
	Nov	1,226			1,158	105.9
			13,961	1,163		
	Dec	1,126			1,166	96.6
			14,018	1,168		
1974	Jan	1,293			1,174	110.1
			14,165	1,180		
	Feb	1,060			1,187	89.3
			14,327	1,194		
	Mar	1,255			1,204	104.2
			14,559	1,213		
	Apr	1,315			1,217	108.1
			14,642	1,220		
	May	1,370			1,220	112.3
			14,630	1,219		
	Jun	1,143			1,221	93.6
			14,668	1,222		
	Jul	1,100			1,218	90.3
			14,562	1,214		
	Aug	1,202			1,212	99.2
			14,520	1,210		
	Sep	1,226			1,202	102.0
			14,314	1,193		
	Oct	1,326			1,187	111.7
			14,171	1,181		

Table 9.5 (*continued*)

	(1) Pork Production	(2) Twelve-Month Moving Total	(3) Twelve-Month Moving Average: col. (2)/12	(4) Centered Twelve-Month Moving Average	(5) Specific Seasonal Indexes
Nov	1,214			1,166	104.1
		13,802	1,150		
Dec	1,164			1,142	101.9
		13,600	1,133		
1975 Jan	1,187			1,124	105.6
		13,364	1,114		
Feb	1,018			1,099	92.6
		13,007	1,084		
Mar	1,049			1,073	97.8
		12,744	1,062		
Apr	1,172			1,049	111.7
		12,420	1,035		
May	1,001			1,025	97.7
		12,183	1,015		
Jun	941			1,011	93.1
		12,077	1,006		
Jul	864			1,000	86.4
		11,914	993		
Aug	845			988	85.5
		11,799	983		
Sep	963			989	97.4
		11,924	994		
Oct	1,002			990	101.2
		11,832	986		
Nov	977			984	99.3
		11,782	982		
Dec	1,058			983	107.6
		11,805	984		
1976 Jan	1,024			986	103.9
		11,855	988		
Feb	903			999	90.4
		12,112	1,009		
Mar	1,174			1,018	115.3
		12,316	1,026		

Table 9.5 (*continued*)

		(1) Pork Production	(2) Twelve-Month Moving Total	(3) Twelve-Month Moving Average: col. (2)/12	(4) Centered Twelve-Month Moving Average	(5) Specific Seasonal Indexes
	Apr	1,080			1,038	104.0
			12,599	1,050		
	May	951			1,066	89.2
			12,969	1,081		
	Jun	964			1,088	88.6
			13,131	1,094		
	Jul	914			1,092	83.7
			13,084	1,090		
	Aug	1,102			1,093	100.8
			13,149	1,096		
	Sep	1,167			1,097	106.4
			13,181	1,098		
	Oct	1,285			1,098	117.0
			13,178	1,098		
	Nov	1,347			1,101	122.3
			13,230	1,103		
	Dec	1,220			1,104	110.5
			13,246	1,104		
1977	Jan	977			1,101	88.7
			13,167	1,097		
	Feb	968			1,095	88.4
			13,098	1,092		
	Mar	1,206			1,089	110.7
			13,021	1,085		
	Apr	1,077			1,078	99.9
			12,843	1,070		
	May	1,003			1,064	94.3
			12,685	1,057		
	Jun	980			1,050	93.3
			12,518	1,043		
	Jul	835			1,045	79.9
			12,547	1,046		
	Aug	1,033			1,046	98.8
			12,551	1,046		

Table 9.5 (*continued*)

		(1) Pork Production	(2) Twelve-Month Moving Total	(3) Twelve-Month Moving Average: col. (2)/12	(4) Centered Twelve-Month Moving Average	(5) Specific Seasonal Indexes
	Sep	1,090			1,043	104.5
			12,480	1,040		
	Oct	1,107			1,039	106.5
			12,456	1,038		
	Nov	1,189			1,042	114.1
			12,536	1,045		
	Dec	1,053			1,046	100.7
			12,563	1,047		
1978	Jan	1,006			1,051	95.7
			12,654	1,055		
	Feb	972			1,056	92.0
			12,681	1,057		
	Mar	1,135			1,056	107.5
			12,648	1,054		
	Apr	1,053			1,055	99.8
			12,674	1,056		
	May	1,083			1,056	102.6
			12,670	1,056		
	Jun	1,007			1,056	95.4
			12,689	1,057		
	Jul	926			1,061	87.3
			12,777	1,065		
	Aug	1,060			1,064	99.6
			12,763	1,064		
	Sep	1,057			1,067	99.1
			12,831	1,069		
	Oct	1,133			1,075	105.4
			12,969	1,081		
	Nov	1,185			1,089	108.8
			13,148	1,096		
	Dec	1,072			1,103	97.2
			13,309	1,109		

Table 9.5 (continued)

		(1) Pork Production	(2) Twelve-Month Moving Total	(3) Twelve-Month Moving Average: col. (2)/12	(4) Centered Twelve-Month Moving Average	(5) Specific Seasonal Indexes
1979	Jan	1,094			1,120	97.7
			13,559	1,130		
	Feb	958			1,140	84.0
			13,801	1,150		
	Mar	1,203			1,155	104.2
			13,903	1,159		
	Apr	1,191			1,174	101.4
			14,262	1,189		
	May	1,262			1,198	105.3
			14,480	1,207		
	Jun	1,168			1,215	96.1
			14,668	1,222		
	Jul	1,176			1,235	95.2
			14,960	1,247		
	Aug	1,302			1,259	103.4
			15,236	1,270		
	Sep	1,159			1,275	90.9
			15,363	1,280		
	Oct	1,492			1,291	115.6
			15,619	1,302		
	Nov	1,403			1,308	107.3
			15,768	1,314		
	Dec	1,260			1,318	95.6
			15,857	1,321		
1980	Jan	1,386			1,322	104.8
			15,862	1,322		
	Feb	1,234			1,316	93.8
			15,702	1,309		
	Mar	1,330			1,314	101.2
			15,828	1,319		
	Apr	1,447			1,317	109.9
			15,765	1,314		

Table 9.5 (*continued*)

	(1) Pork Production	(2) Twelve-Month Moving Total	(3) Twelve-Month Moving Average: col. (2)/12	(4) Centered Twelve-Month Moving Average	(5) Specific Seasonal Indexes
May	1,411			1,309	107.8
		15,643	1,304		
Jun	1,257			1,308	96.1
		15,741	1,312		
Jul	1,181				
Aug	1,142				
Sep	1,285				
Oct	1,429				
Nov	1,281				
Dec	1,358				

necessary to derive the ratio to moving average method seasonal index. The first column is simply a sequential listing of the pork production figures found in Table 9.1.

The second step is to total the pork production for 1971 and center that in the middle of 1971. Because the total pork production was 15,989 million pounds and since the middle of 1971 occurs between June and July, the twelve-month total is placed on the line between June and July. The next figure in the column is derived by subtracting the production for January 1971 and adding the production for January 1982. This total of 15,789 is placed between July and August of 1971. It is placed there because that is the midpoint in the twelve months starting February 1971 and ending January 1972. The analyst continues with this procedure of subtracting the oldest month in the twelve months and adding the next new month. This total, as always, is placed at the midpoint of the particular twelve months being totaled. This procedure continues to the end of the ten-year period.

The third step is to compute a twelve-month moving average. This is found by dividing the figure in column 2 by 12, the months in the year. Thus the initial figure of 1,332 is the monthly average for the twelve months in 1971. It was derived by dividing the twelve-month moving total in column 2 of 15,989 by twelve months. The twelve-month moving average is placed to the right of the twelve-month moving total. Thus it is also between June and July. The analyst proceeds to divide each twelve-month moving total in column 2 by 12 and places the result in column 3. The next step is to center the twelve-month moving average. This fourth step is done by averaging the twelve-month moving averages in column 3 above and below the relevant month. For example, the analyst wishes to center the twelve-month moving average of July. He takes the twelve-month moving average of 1,332 and 1,316, adds them together and divides by 2. The 1,332 and 1,316 are the twelve-month moving averages directly above and below the line for July 1971. This particular average 1,324, is placed directly on the same line as July 1971. Each successive entry in column 4 is simply the average of the two values directly above and below the particular month that the centered moving average is placed on. The analyst should proceed to finding these averages for each of the months for the ten years.

Then step five is to derive the specific seasonal indexes for each year. This is done by dividing the number in column 1 by the number in column 4. Our first example, July 1971, is 1,157 divided by the centered twelve-month moving average of 1,324. The result, 87.4, is placed on the July 1971 line in column 5. Note again that we multiply the result by 100. This same procedure is followed through each of the months for the complete ten years. We have now found how the particular month in a given twelve-month period related to the average monthly for the whole twelve-month period.

The next step is to collect the specific seasonal indexes into a typical seasonal index for the whole ten-year period. The easiest way to accomplish this task is to construct a table of the specific seasonal indexes found in column 5. A Table 9.6 has been constructed for our pork production example. Notice that there are no specific seasonals for the first six months of 1971 and the last six months of 1980. This is due to the method of using the twelve-month moving total centered in the middle of the year.

The next step is to total the numbers in each of the columns. This

Table 9.6 Specific Seasonal Indexes for Pork Production

	Jan	Feb	Mar	Apr	May	Jun	Jul	Aug	Sep	Oct	Nov	Dec	Total
1971							87.4	95.7	102.8	101.2	109.6	109.5	
1972	92.7	90.4	114.5	99.7	102.4	97.2	80.5	97.9	96.8	109.5	112.0	98.5	
1973	105.1	90.1	106.6	97.2	110.1	96.3	84.3	91.7	87.6	108.6	105.9	96.6	
1974	110.1	89.3	104.2	108.1	112.3	93.6	90.3	99.2	102.0	111.7	104.1	101.9	
1975	105.6	92.6	97.8	111.7	97.7	93.1	86.4	85.5	97.4	101.2	99.3	107.6	
1976	103.9	90.4	115.3	104.0	89.2	88.6	83.7	100.8	106.4	117.0	122.3	110.5	
1977	88.7	88.4	110.7	99.9	94.3	93.3	79.9	98.8	104.5	106.5	114.1	100.7	
1978	95.7	92.0	107.5	99.8	102.6	95.4	87.3	99.6	99.1	105.4	108.8	97.2	
1979	97.7	84.0	104.2	101.4	105.3	96.1	95.2	103.4	90.9	115.6	107.3	95.6	
1980	104.8	93.8	101.2	109.9	107.8	96.1							
Total[a]	705.5	633.2	748.9	722.8	720.2	663.9	599.9	683.7	693.5	758.5	761.8	712.0	
Modified mean	100.8	90.5	107.0	103.3	102.9	94.8	85.7	97.7	99.1	108.4	108.8	101.7	1,200.7
Typical index	100.7	90.4	106.9	103.2	102.8	94.7	85.7	97.6	99.0	108.3	108.7	101.6	1,199.6

[a] After deleting the highest and lowest values.

time, however, we are going to eliminate from our totaling the highest and lowest values in each column. This will take out some of the possible distortions caused by an exceptional value. Thus, for example, in the January column, the 110.1 and 88.7 are eliminated before the column is totaled. Therefore, each column is the total of only seven years. The row under the total is a modified mean. This is the total divided by the number of months that were totaled, in this example, seven. Thus 705.5, the total of the January column divided by 7, equals 100.8 as the modified mean for January. It is called the modified mean because the two extreme values were deleted. The modified means are totaled to discover how much rounding error has been found in the adding and averaging process. In this example, the total of all the modified means is 1,200.7. Theoretically, the total should be equal to 1,200.0. Because of rounding errors we have found a slight difference from the theoretical value.

One way to make the total slightly more accurate is to adjust the modified mean by a correction factor. The correction factor is simply the theoretical total of the modified means, 1,200, divided by the actual total of the modified means, 1,200.7. This correction factor, .9994, is multiplied by each of the various modified means to derive the typical seasonal index. Notice that the correction is slight compared to the modified mean. In most cases the index has been shifted down only .1. The total of the typical seasonal indexes, 1,199.6, is only marginally closer to the theoretical total of 1,200.00 than the original total of the modified means, 1,200.7. Thus in some cases the last step in the procedure might not be worth the time and effort. In other cases, however, there will be a significant improvement in accuracy if the analyst takes the final step.

It can be seen that the ratio to moving average technique provides significantly more accuracy at the cost of more time. The additional time, however, may be reduced by the use of computers or programmable calculators.

Nonetheless, both methods of deriving a seasonal index can be applied to many facets of the spread trading program. It can be used, as in this example, to derive a seasonal index for certain factors which affect spread values. It can also be applied directly to spread prices. This is probably the most common approach that traders make. There are several published books which give the seasonality of various spread combinations (listed in Chapter 16). The trader is urged to examine these books.

Seasonal analysis is a powerful tool in the spread traders quest for profits. It can provide spread ideas, generate confirmations, and keep the trader out of potentially bad trades.

TEN

Regression
and Correlation
Analysis

Regression and correlation analysis applies statistical techniques to
spread trading. Don't worry—it's much easier than it sounds. Don't
be put off by the math or mathematical symbols. Even if you can't tell
a standard deviation from a correlation coefficient, this chapter will
show you how to use simple statistical techniques to trade spreads.

Regression analysis is concerned with the prediction of one number
based on the knowledge of another number. Put another way, it is the
prediction of one variable, called the *dependent variable*, based on a
second variable, the *independent variable*. A variable is simply a number. Notice that we want to predict a dependent variable. It is called
the dependent variable because it depends on the other variable, the
independent variable.

We will also look at correlation analysis. This shows whether there
is a relationship between two sets of numbers and, if so, how related
the two sets are.

REGRESSION ANALYSIS

The aim of regression analysis is to predict one number based on a second number. There are also tests that will give us an idea of how much accuracy we have.

The first step in using regression analysis is to set up a scatter diagram, which is a chart of the two numbers under consideration. To draw a scatter diagram the analyst puts one variable on the left side of the chart, called the *Y*-axis, and places the second variable across the bottom of the chart, called the *X*-axis.

Let's assume that an analyst wishes to predict the price of the July/November soybean spread as of July 1 of each year. The analyst theorizes that the July/November soybean spread on July 1 may be related to the ratio of old crop ending stocks versus new crop production. Since the July contract is in the old crop and the November is in the new crop, the analyst surmises that this spread will largely reflect the relative supply and demand of the two different crop years. Since ending stocks are a measure of the supply and demand in the old crop and new crop production is the major factor in the new crop supply and demand, the analyst assumes that there is a relation between the stocks and production that may have some bearing on the July/November soybean spread. It is through regression analysis that the relation between the ratio and the price can be determined.

The analyst must collect three pieces of information:

1. The ending stocks of the years under review.
2. The production of the year following the year of the ending stocks.
3. The price of the July/November soybean spread on July 1.

The trader decides that fifteen years ought to be a reasonable number to examine. He collects the crop production and ending stock figures by thumbing through U.S. Department of Agriculture reports or by looking through a couple of copies of the *Commodity Yearbook* published by the Commodity Research Bureau. He places the data into a table (Table 10.1).

The second step is to plot the information onto a scatter diagram. After the analyst has done this he has constructed a diagram like Figure 10.1. With the exception of the two points indicated by ar-

Table 10.1   July/November Soybean Spread Information

	Ending Stocks (millions of bushels)	Production of Following Year	End Stocks/ Production of Following Year	Jul/Nov Bean Spread Price
1964/65	29.7	845.6	.035	+50
1965/66	35.6	928.5	.038	+55
1966/67	89.7	976.4	.092	+10
1967/68	166.3	1,107.0	.150	+10
1968/69	326.8	1,133.1	.288	+31
1969/70	229.8	1,127.1	.204	+4
1970/71	98.8	1,176.1	.084	+5
1971/72	72.0	1,270.6	.057	+24
1972/73	59.6	1,547.5	.039	+150
1973/74	170.9	1,216.3	.141	−2
1974/75	188.2	1,547.4	.122	+11
1975/76	244.8	1,287.6	.190	−13
1976/77	102.9	1,761.8	.058	+50
1977/78	161.0	1,870.2	.086	+50
1978/79	174.4	2,267.6	.077	+15

rows, a line can be drawn through the area where most of the points appear. Thus there seems to be some kind of relation between the ratio and the price. If the scatter diagram had instead looked like Figure 10.2, it would be hard to believe that there was a relationship between the two variables.

The analyst hopes to find a scatter diagram where all the points fall on a single line (see Figure 10.3). This would show a perfect relationship between the two variables. However, reality is not perfect. A more common pattern is the one in Figure 10.4. The points are scattered, but they appear to cluster around the central line. Figure 10.5 shows points which run around the central line but appear to be farther away. Thus Figure 10.4 would probably get the analyst's attention more readily than Figure 10.5.

If the analyst has been able to construct a scatter diagram similar to Figure 10.1, he has a good candidate for regression analysis. On the other hand, if he finds a plot like Figure 10.2, the analyst should try another theory.

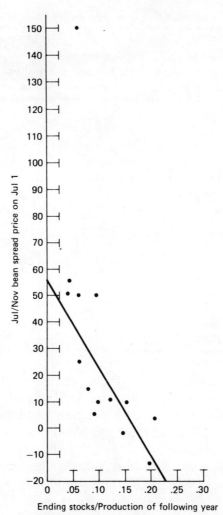

Figure 10.1 Spread information scatter diagram.

A linear regression equation is simply an equation that describes the line that goes through the group of points. It is sometimes called a regression equation, a predicting equation, or an estimating equation. Although it would be possible to draw a line freehand on the chart and use that freehand line as a prediction device, it is better to go through the math and come up with something more precise and useful.

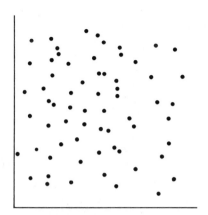

Figure 10.2   Scatter diagram.

The regression equation is determined by using a mathematical method called the least squares method. This method gives us the line that best fits the points on the graph. By best fitting line, we mean the line that is the closest to all the points on the chart.

The process of linear regression is to come up with an estimating equation that looked like this:

$$\overline{Y}_P = a + bX \qquad (1)$$

Don't let that equation scare you. It may look a little unusual but it's really simple. It's just a shorthand way of expressing something that

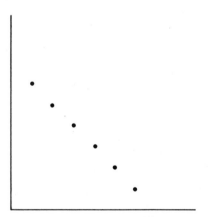

Figure 10.3   Scatter diagram.

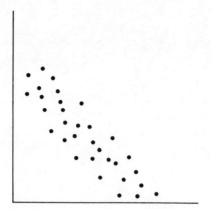

Figure 10.4   Scatter diagram.

might take a long sentence to express. Let's look at each of the elements of the equation.

The Y in the equation is the symbol for the variable Y. The variable Y is the variable that goes down the vertical axis of the scatter diagram. The subscript P beside the Y means that it is the predicted value of Y. The bar that sits on top of the Y is the symbol for average. See—that's not so hard.

The Y intercept is the symbol a. In plain English, this is the estimated value of the variable Y when the variable X equals zero. Another way to put it is that a is where the regression line crosses the Y axis, which is the vertical axis.

Figure 10.5   Scatter diagram.

The slope of the regression line is the symbol b. This is the average change in $\overline{Y}_p$ for each change of one unit of the variable X.

X is the value of the variable that the analyst uses to predict the value of the variable Y.

If you look at Figure 10.1, the a, which is the point where the line starts on the Y-axis, was set at about 55. The b, or slope of the line, is the slope of the drawn line. If the dots had been placed at a different part of the chart, the line could be slanted or sloped in many different directions. In Figure 10.1, the slope of the line is considered negative. That is because the line goes from the upper left to the lower right. If the line went from the lower left to the upper right, it would be called a positive slope.

The regression equation just outlined usually does not give an exact description of the relationship between the variables X and Y. The only case where it would be an exact description would be if all the points in the scatter diagram were in a single line, similar to that shown in Figure 10.3. Because this is a rare circumstance, the regression equation is usually considered to be an estimate of the relation between the variables X and Y. The values a and b are therefore called the estimated regression coefficients. Usually, though, they are simply referred to as the regression coefficients. That equation (equation 1) is where we want to be. We want to find out what the regression coefficients a and b are. Once we have those two coefficients, we can use the equation to predict the price of spreads.

There are a couple of ways that the regression coefficients can be determined. By determining the regression coefficients we are building the equation for the regression line. The method that I find easiest is to solve the following two equations:

$$b = \frac{n(\Sigma XY) - (\Sigma X)(\Sigma Y)}{n(\Sigma X^2) - (\Sigma X)^2} \tag{2}$$

$$a = \frac{\Sigma Y}{n} - b\,\frac{\Sigma X}{n} \quad \text{or} \quad \overline{Y} - b\overline{X} \tag{3}$$

Hold on! Don't panic! These two equations may look more complicated than the first equation but they, too, are really quite simple.

These equations introduce the symbol that looks like a crooked E. This is the Greek letter sigma. It simply means the sum of a group of numbers. When you add 2 and 2 you get the sum of 4. If we substituted an X for the number 2, then ΣX would mean the addition of all the X's. This will probably become clearer in the example that follows.

The second thing that we have added in these two equations is the concept of squaring a number. When one sees a small "2" above and to the right of a number or letter, that is the symbol for squaring the number or letter. We say that X^2, or X squared, is simply X multiplied by itself. Thus 5^2 is the same as 5×5 or 25. Similarly, X^2 simply means X times X.

To solve these equations we construct a table which is very similar to Table 10.1 except that we have added two additional columns (see Table 10.2). This time we have placed an X over the column that contains the ratio of ending stocks to a new crop production. If you remember, this ratio was the X-axis on the scatter diagram. We have also placed a Y over the column of the July 1 price of the July/Nov bean spread because this is the column which represents the Y-axis in the scatter diagram.

The two new columns are labeled X^2 and XY. The X^2 column is the number which represents the ratio X times itself. For example, the ratio of end stocks to new crop production in 1964/65 was .035. When one multiplies this ratio by itself, $.035 \times .035$, the result is .0012. This is the number which has been placed in the X^2 column for the year 1964/65.

The column labeled XY is even simpler to understand. The column XY represents the multiplication of the ratio X times the price Y. In the year 1964/65, if one multiplies the ratio X, ending stocks divided by new crop production, times the price on July 1, column Y, one gets 1.75. This value is placed in the XY column.

Notice that we have not placed values in the X^2 and XY columns for 1968/69 and 1972/73. These two years represent years which were very much out of the ordinary; they are the points noted by arrows in Figure 10.1. In each of these two years something happened to throw the normal relation between the ratio and the price out of whack. Thus when we solve this equation we will be finding the regression equation which best describes those years in which some semblance of normalcy prevailed. It can be argued that the spread analyst should

Table 10.2 July/November Soybean Spread Information

	End Stocks/ (millions of bushels)	Production of Following Year	X End Stocks/ Production of Following Year	Y Jul/Nov Bean Spread Price	X^2	XY
1964/65	29.7	845.6	.035	+50	.0012	1.75
1965/66	35.6	928.5	.038	+55	.0014	2.09
1966/67	89.7	976.4	.092	+10	.0085	.92
1967/68	166.3	1,107.0	.150	+10	.0225	1.50
1968/69	326.8	1,133.1	.288	+31	—	—
1969/70	229.8	1,127.1	.204	+4	.0416	.816
1970/71	98.8	1,176.1	.084	+5	.0071	.42
1971/72	72.0	1,270.6	.057	+24	.0032	1.368
1972/73	59.6	1,547.5	.039	+150	—	—
1973/74	170.9	1,216.3	.141	−2	.0199	−.282
1974/75	188.2	1,547.4	.122	+11	.0149	.342
1975/76	244.8	1,287.6	.190	−13	.0361	−2.47
1976/77	102.9	1,761.8	.058	+50	.0034	2.90
1977/78	161.0	1,870.2	.086	+50	.0074	4.30
1978/79	174.4	2,267.6	.077	+16	.0059	1.155
Total			1.344	+269	.1731	15.809

develop a regression equation which takes into account the two anomaly years. However, when there are only one or two anomalies, it is usually better to eliminate them from the analysis. It is then the responsibility of the analyst to recognize that particular year that comes along every ten years in which the regression equation will not work. The regression equation should instead be developed for use during "normal" years.

At the bottom of the columns labeled X, Y, X^2, and XY are the totals of the numbers in each column. The number .1731 at the bottom of the column labeled X^2 is the sum of X^2 of all the years. This could be expressed, in mathematical notation, as ΣX^2. As another example, ΣXY is 15.809, which represents the addition of all the numbers in the column labeled XY.

The n in the formulas is the number of points that we are examining. In our example, we are looking at the years 1964/65 to 1978/79. That's fifteen years, but since we are eliminating the years 1968/69 and 1972/73, our n in this example is 13.

Thus we can give values to the symbols in equations 2 and 3. ΣXY is 15.809, ΣX is 1.334, ΣY is 269, and ΣX^2 is .1731. To obtain ΣX^2, the analyst has to take ΣX, 1.334, and multiply it by itself. Thus ΣX^2 is 1.1780. From now on everything is simple arithmetic. Let's follow the example through:

$$b = \frac{n(\Sigma XY) - (\Sigma X)(\Sigma Y)}{n(\Sigma X^2) - (\Sigma X)^2}$$

$$b = \frac{13(15.809) - (1.334)(269)}{13(.1731) - (1.334)^2}$$

$$b = \frac{205.517 - 358.846}{2.2503 - 1.7796}$$

$$b = \frac{-153.329}{.4707}$$

$$b = -325.75$$

$$a = \frac{\Sigma Y}{n} - \left(b \, \frac{\Sigma X}{n}\right)$$

$$a = \frac{269}{13} - \left(-325.75 \times \frac{1.334}{13}\right)$$

$$a = 20.69 - (-33.43)$$

$$a = 54.12$$

We have discovered that the regression coefficient a is equal to 54.12 and the regression coefficient b is equal to -325.75. Thus our regression equation looks like

$$\overline{Y}_P = 54.12 - 325.75X \qquad (4)$$

The analyst is now in a position to predict the price of the July/November soybean spread on July 1. She must still predict what the ending stocks are going to be in the current crop year as well as predict the production in the coming crop year, but this is typically easier than trying to predict the price. The trader always has the option to rely on those whose job it is to predict stocks and production. The trader can utilize the services of the U.S. Department of Agriculture in their supply and demand estimates and prospective planting reports, or the spread trader can utilize private sources such as a broker or newsletter.

For example, on April 15, the spread trader looks at the latest supply and demand projection issued by the U.S.D.A. The U.S.D.A. has predicted that soybean ending stocks will be 200 million bushels. The trader also examines the last U.S.D.A. Prospective Plantings Report to find the U.S.D.A. estimate of how many acres of soybeans will be planted. Using an average yield for the past five years, the trader multiplies the prospective planting acreage by the average yield and determines that 2 billion bushels is a likely crop production figure. By dividing the ending stocks of 200 million by the estimated new crop production of 2 billion, the trader obtains the ratio X of .100. By substituting that in equation 4 she can obtain the predicted value of the July/November soybean spread on July 1. The math looks like this:

$$\overline{Y}_P = 54.12 - 325.75(.100)$$

$$\overline{Y}_P = 54.12 - 32.575$$

$$\overline{Y}_P = 21.54$$

The trader thus has predicted that the price of July/November soybeans will be approximately 21½ cents on July 1. This is equivalent to saying that the price of July soybeans will be 21½ cents higher than the price of November soybeans.

If, on April 15, the July contract is already about 21½ cents over the November contract, the trader will realize that there is probably no significant opportunity for profit. On the other hand, should July soybeans be 10 cents below the price of November soybeans, there is a potential for the spread to move more than 30 cents from April 15 to July 1. All other things being equal, the spread trader would then be in a position to initiate a long July/short November soybean spread with the expectation of a significant profit.

HOW ACCURATE IS THE PREDICTION?

Unfortunately, our statistical tea leaf is not 100% accurate. In fact, any trader should be surprised if such a prediction came true. The object of any trading method is to make more money on the profitable trades than you lose on the unprofitable trades. Though the estimating equation isn't perfect, it can lead to profitable trades.

Still, the question arises: How accurate is the equation? If the equation were 100% accurate, the trader would mortgage the family farm and put on the trade. If the equation was accurate only 10% of the time, the trader can easily conclude that he had just wasted his time developing the numbers.

But what if the trader develops coefficients that look pretty good? Can the trader predict how accurate his predictions are going to be?

The speculator can predict the equation's accuracy by determining the standard error of estimate. The standard error of estimate simply gives the basic range around an estimate that the trader can be reasonably sure represents an accurate prediction. In other words, a given equation may predict a July/October sugar price of 123 points premium October, give or take 46 points.

The object of using the standard error of estimating is to find a range of values that the trader is 95% sure the price will eventually enter. The trader would have 95% confidence in this estimated range.

One can look at it in another way. The trader must assume that the relationship between the fundamental indicator and the price will remain the same in the future as it has in the past. Given this assumption, the trader will be able to say that, based on his estimate of the fundamental indicator, 95% of the time the predicted price will fall in a particular range.

The Standard Error of Estimate

The equation to determine the standard error of estimate is

$$S_{x \cdot y} = \sqrt{\frac{\Sigma Y^2 - a(\Sigma Y) - b(\Sigma XY)}{\lambda - 2}} \tag{5}$$

Just relax. This one's easier than the last one. In fact, you've already got it partially figured out.

We're going to bring back Table 10.2, this time adding one more column to the end. That column, labeled Y^2, is the price on July 1 times itself. If the price on July 1 is +50, then Y^2 is +2,500. Don't forget that a minus number multiplied by itself is a positive number. In 1975/76, the July 1 price was −13, but Y^2 was +169.

By taking the numbers in Table 10.3 and substituting them for their algebraic names in equation 5, we can solve for the range which gives 68% accuracy. To obtain 95% of the range we need to multiply the results by 1.96 and, if we really want to get confident and enclose 99.7% within the range, we would multiply the result of the equation by 3.

Confidence Limits

We have shown how to set up confidence limits around a predicted price. This formula, equation 5, is the proper equation to use to determine confidence limits and need not be adjusted if the sample of data is large. Any samples numbering over 150 should be considered large. If your sample of data is smaller, then we need to add yet another equation to adjust equation 5 for the smallness of the sample.

We must correct the errors which may have occurred due to a small sample. The correcting equation is

$$\overline{Y}_P \pm t(S_{y \cdot x}) \sqrt{\frac{1}{n} + \frac{(x - \bar{x})^2}{\Sigma(x - \bar{x})^2}} \qquad (6)$$

Thus far you've met all of the symbols in this equation with the exception of the lowercase t right after the $+$ or $-$ symbol. The t is the value of t from the Table of Critical Values of t listed in the appendix to this book. The value that we should select from the appendix is for 3 degrees of freedom.

This formula corrects and compensates for the error of the estimating equation and also for the sampling error. Each trader should try to obtain as large a sample as possible to decrease the amount of potential error.

Let's plug in the numbers of our current example and see how much the confidence limit is adjusted:

$$\overline{Y}_P \pm t(S_{y \cdot x}) \sqrt{\frac{1}{n} + \frac{(x - \bar{x})^2}{\Sigma(x - \bar{x})^2}}$$

$$16 \pm 2.16(14.93) \sqrt{.0769 + \frac{(.117 - .103)^2}{.0013}}$$

$$16 \pm 32.25\sqrt{.0769 + .1508}$$

$$16 \pm 32.25\sqrt{.2277}$$

$$16 \pm 32.25(.4771)$$

$$16 \pm 15.3865$$

Table 10.3 July/November Soybean Spread Information

	End Stocks (millions of bushels)	X		Y	X²	XY	Y²
		Production of Following Year	End Stocks/ Production of Following Year	Jul/Nov Bean Spread Price			
1964/65	29.7	845.6	.035	+50	.0012	1.75	2,500
1965/66	35.6	928.5	.038	+55	.0014	2.09	3,025
1966/67	89.7	976.4	.092	+10	.0085	.92	100
1967/68	166.3	1,107.0	.150	+10	.0225	1.50	100
1968/69	326.8	1,133.1	.288	+31	—	—	—
1969/70	229.8	1,127.1	.204	+4	.0416	.816	16
1970/71	98.8	1,176.1	.084	+5	.0071	.42	25
1971/72	72.0	1,270.6	.057	+24	.0032	1.368	576
1972/73	59.6	1,547.5	.039	+150	—	—	—
1973/74	170.9	1,216.3	.141	−2	.0199	−.282	4
1974/75	188.2	1,547.4	.122	+11	.0149	1.342	121
1975/76	244.8	1,287.6	.190	−13	.0361	−2.47	169
1976/77	102.9	1,761.8	.058	+50	.0034	2.90	2,500
1977/78	161.0	1,870.2	.086	+50	.0074	4.30	2,500
1978/79	174.4	2,267.6	.077	+16	.0059	1.155	225
Total			1.344	269	.1731	15.809	11,861

Table 10.4 July/November Soybean Spread Information

	End Stocks (millions of bushels)	Production of Following Year	X End Stocks/ Production of Following Year	Y Jul/Nov Bean Spread Price	X^2	XY	Y^2	$(x - \bar{x})^2$
1964/65	29.7	845.6	.035	+50	.0012	1.75	2,500	.0046
1965/66	35.6	928.5	.038	+55	.0014	2.09	3,025	.0042
1966/67	89.7	976.4	.092	+10	.0085	.92	100	.0001
1967/68	166.3	1,107.0	.150	+10	.0225	1.50	100	.0022
1968/69	326.8	1,133.1	.288	+31	—	—	—	—
1969/70	229.8	1,127.1	.204	+4	.0416	.816	16	.0103
1970/71	98.8	1,176.1	.084	+5	.0071	.42	25	.0003
1971/72	72.0	1,270.6	.057	+24	.0032	1.368	576	.0021
1972/73	59.6	1,547.5	.039	+150	—	—	—	—
1973/74	170.9	1,216.3	.141	−2	.0199	−.282	4	.0015
1974/75	188.2	1,547.4	.122	+11	.0149	1.342	121	.0004
1975/76	244.8	1,287.6	.190	−13	.0361	−2.47	169	.0076
1976/77	102.9	1,761.8	.058	+50	.0034	2.90	2,500	.0020
1977/78	161.0	1,870.2	.086	+50	.0074	4.30	2,500	.0003
1978/79	174.4	2,267.6	.077	+16	.0059	1.155	225	.0007
Total			1.344	269	.1731	15.809	11,861	.0363

Also in the small sample correcting equation we have added the potentially confusing symbol of $X - \overline{X}$. We'll bring back Table 10.3 and add one more column on the end to give $(X - \overline{X})^2$. We have already told you what X is. $\overline{X}$ is simply the mean or the average of the X's. If you take X, 1.334, and divide it by the 13 numbers in our sample you get $\overline{X}$, or .103. Our new column takes the x for a particular year, subtracts the average for all the years, and then multiplies that result by itself.

CORRELATION ANALYSIS

The point of correlation analysis is to try to find what portion of the price is determined by our fundamental indicator and what portion is not determined by it. Each price, which must be related to fundamental factors, is determined by explained variation and unexplained variation.

If our example was able to explain 72% of the variation in price, we would say that 72% of the price of July/November soybeans on July 1 is explained by the change in the fundamental indicator, ending stocks divided by the new crop production.

The portion of the variation which is explained is called the *coefficient of determination*, or r^2. The unexplained variation is cleverly called the *coefficient of nondetermination*, or $1 - r^2$. The coefficient of determination can be any value from 0 to 1. A coefficient of determination with a value of 0 means that none of the variation in the price is explained by the fundamental indicator. In mathematical language it indicates that none of the variation in Y is explained by the X variable. Conversely, a coefficient of 1 indicates that all of the variation in Y is explained by X. In our example, a coefficient of 1 would mean that you will always be able to know the July/November soybean value on July 1 if you know the supply/demand numbers.

It is very rare to find a correlation of 0 or 1. Most frequently the coefficient of determination lies somewhere between the two extremes. It is always the goal of the analyst to discover highly correlated pieces of information. The higher the correlation, the more confidence the trader can put in the projection.

To find the coefficient of determination the analyst must first find the correlation coefficient. The correlation coefficient, designated by

r, is merely the square root of the coefficient of determination. The following equation gives the correlation coefficient:

$$r = \frac{\lambda(\Sigma XY) - (\Sigma X)(\Sigma Y)}{\sqrt{[n(\Sigma X^2) - (\Sigma X)^2][n(\Sigma Y^2) - (\Sigma Y)^2]}} \qquad (7)$$

Believe it or not, of the equations so far outlined, this is the easiest to solve. We have already discovered all of the values that are needed to use this equation. We merely have to plug them in and use simple arithmetic to get the answer. Let's carry on our example, plug in the numbers, and see what we get:

$$r = \frac{n(\Sigma XY) - (\Sigma X)(\Sigma Y)}{\sqrt{[n(\Sigma X^2) - (\Sigma X)^2][n(\Sigma Y^2) - (\Sigma Y)^2]}}$$

$$r = \frac{13(15.809) - (1.334)(269)}{\sqrt{(13(.1731) - (1.334)^2)(13(11861) - (269)^2)}}$$

$$r = \frac{205.517 - 358.846}{\sqrt{(2.2503 - 1.7796)(154193 - 72361)}}$$

$$r = \frac{-153.329}{\sqrt{38518.322}}$$

$$r = \frac{-153.329}{196.261}$$

$$r = -.78$$

$$r^2 = .61$$

The common practice is to round off the result r to the nearest hundredth. Thus in this example, r would be -0.78. This value, the correlation coefficient, tells us whether there is a positive or negative relationship between the indicator and the price. Because r is a minus number, the relation is negative. As one gets larger the other gets smaller and vice versa. An example of negative correlation would be cattle slaughter versus cattle prices. As cattle slaughter gets larger, cattle prices get smaller. A positive correlation is one in which each of the numbers goes in the same direction. As the indicator goes up the price goes up. If soybean exports get larger, the price of soybeans gets larger.

To discover what portion of the price variation that you have discovered using this indicator, you square the correlation coefficient r and derive the coefficient of determination. In the example above, $-.78$ times itself equals an r^2 of .61. In other words, 61% of the variation of the July/November soybean spread price on July 1 is explained by the variation in the fundamental indicator of ending stocks divided by new crop production. This is a pretty good coefficient of determination and is quite usable by the spread trader as an indicator of prices.

HOW TO USE THE ESTIMATING EQUATION

After the trader has found a relationship that appears accurate and valid, the trader must use the equation to develop profitable trades. There are two basic ways to use the equations. The trader can estimate the value of a particular spread at a particular time in the future or she can evaluate the prices of the two contracts separately.

An example of the first type of use is the July/November soybean equation above. The analyst first ascertains the value of the spread at some point in the future. If the expected future value is significantly different from the current value, the trader has the possibility of a trade. For example, the July/November soybean equation says that, given the expected fundamentals, the price of the July/November soybean spread will be 30¢ premium the July contract on July 1. If the current price is 10¢ premium the November, the trader will have good reason to initiate a long July/short November soybean spread.

The second use is to develop an equation for estimating the prices of the two separate outright contracts. This is particularly applicable to intercommodity spreads and spreads in livestock. In both instances, the separate fundamentals of the two contracts or commodities are more important than the relationship between them.

The trader would develop two separate equations, one for each of the two contracts or commodities. After plugging the fundamentals into the separate equations, the spread trader would have price estimates for each of the two contracts. This gives him a predicted spread differential based on the expected fundamentals and the use of the equations. If this expected differential is significantly different from the current differential, the trader has the potential for a trade.

Notice that each possible use is directed toward estimating the future price of the spread. This gives the trader the price objective of the spread but not how or when to enter or exit. He will have to rely on other techniques in this book to determine his entry and exit points. Nonetheless, the ability to determine underlying value can be a major advantage to the spread trader.

ELEVEN

Chart Analysis

Chart analysis of spreads is the study of the spread price patterns rather than of the supply and demand factors for the cash commodities. Chart analysts further believe that price patterns have a predictive value. The assumption is that people and hence markets follow a certain pattern. These patterns occur and recur as the market participants repeat their behavior patterns.

A chartist believes that the recurrence of these price patterns can be utilized profitably. The price action is underlying the market and the market is the final arbiter of the value of the supply and demand factors. The chart trader is particularly looking for price trends. These would be times when the fundamentals are moving the spread price in a particular direction. Through chart analysis, the trader can ascertain when prices are in a trend and when the trend is over.

The trader can also use chart analysis to discover breakouts. A breakout is a price movement out of a previous trading range. An upside breakout, for example, occurs when the buying pressure becomes greater than the selling pressure. This usually happens when a change occurs in the underlying fundamentals.

Although chart analysis can be used as the sole rationale for a trade, its usual purpose is as an aid in determining entry and exit points. The spread trader would develop a trading idea based on other techniques and could rely on the chart analysis to guide him in where to place initiation and liquidation orders.

Because chart analysis is devoted to the ebb and flow of human behavior, it is better suited to discovering areas of support and resistance in which to initiate and liquidate positions.

119

CHART PATTERNS

Whatever purpose chart analysis is put to, a basic understanding of the most popular chart patterns is a necessity. One problem is that spread charting is done only with closing prices, whereas the typical price chart for an outright contract would contain the high, low, and settlement prices. Thus the spread trader is at a disadvantage. He has no way of knowing what the actual high was in the spread trading in a given day for a given move. The closing price may actually be distorted from the reality of what the spread was trading for. Thus the picture given by a spread chart is not as accurate as that given by the outright bar chart.

The chart analyst also does not have the potential of using point and figure charts. Although services exist which graph point and figure charts for the outright trader, no such service exists for spreads. This is easy to understand when one considers that the chart service would have to have a record of every spread to make such a chart. This is difficult information to obtain in a utilizable form.

Chart analysis (in fact, all technical analyses) has been little used in the analysis of spreads. No articles have ever been published on technical trading systems applied to spreads. The point is that technical analysis rarely has been studied in relation to spreads. This chapter focuses on the major chart patterns because of the author's extensive use of them.

THE MAJOR PATTERNS

One of the significant patterns that every spread trader must learn is the *uptrend line* or *downtrend line*. An uptrend is defined as a price pattern in which each successive low is higher than the previous low and each successive high is higher than the preceding high. A downtrend is the opposite: each low is lower than the previous low and the highs are continually lower.

An uptrend line is drawn along the bottom of the successively higher lows. A downtrend line is a line drawn across the successively lower highs in a downtrend. An example of a downtrend line is seen in Figure 11.1. The highs in January, February, and March are all

50 pts = $562

Figure 11.1   Sugar spread downtrend line.

121

connected by the downtrend line. As prices move downward, they are never able to move upward and penetrate through the downtrend line. The bear spreaders in sugar are obviously in control. Whenever the bull spreaders can rally prices, the bear spreaders are able to move the price down at successively lower values. The downtrend line connects the tops of these down movements and provides resistance to any up moves attempted by bull spreaders.

An uptrend line is the reverse of a downtrend line. The bull spreaders are in control. As bear spreaders try to push the price down, the bull spreaders show their superior force and do not allow the price to move back to the preceding level. The general tendency of the spread is to move upward as the bull spreaders apply more pressure. Two examples of uptrend lines are seen in Figure 11.2. The uptrend line formed by the April, May, and June lows is an example of an uptrend which has provided substantial support to the movement of the July/October live hog spread.

A trend line is considered to be valid until the price breaks through the line. The April through June uptrend line is an example of a successful uptrend line in that it has yet to be broken. The January and February uptrend line, however, was broken during the last week in February. By definition, this means that the uptrend is over and that a consolidation, or downtrend, has begun.

A trend line gains validity the more times it is touched by the price. A trend line can be formed by any two highs or lows. The April through June hog spread uptrend was touched four times by the trend line. Traders can use the trend lines to provide entry and exit points. In the example of the April through June uptrend line, the trader would draw the line after the second low had been reached at the beginning of May. She would then have bought July and sold October hogs when the spread price reacted back down to the uptrend line. She would have liquidated the spread had the price broken through the uptrend line. This would have been a signal that the uptrend was over and that a potential downtrend had begun.

In this example, however, a breakdown did not occur. The price rallied into the beginning of June. A quick one-week retracement dropped the spread value down to the uptrend line where support entered and prevented the spread from trading lower. Prices then took off again and the spread trader would still be holding her July/

100 pts = $300

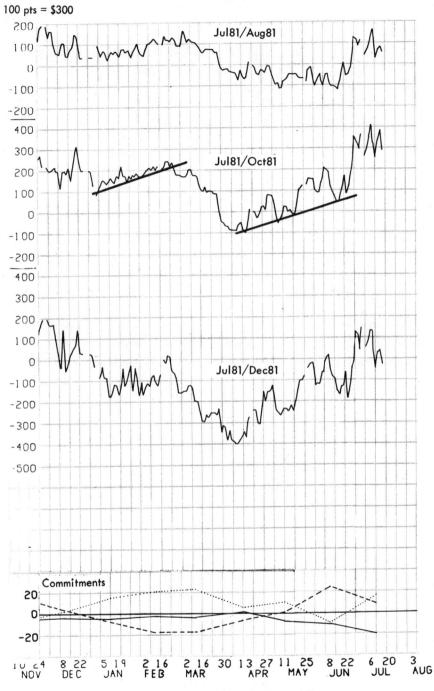

Figure 11.2   Hog spread uptrend line.

123

October hog spread. Note that because the uptrend line is pointed upward the liquidation points move higher every day. It becomes, in effect, a trailing stop behind the price of the spread.

But what would have happened with the January/February uptrend line? The spreader would have entered the position near the end of January and held it until the price of the spread broke down through the uptrend line near the end of February. Because the price had not moved very far, the trader probably would have made only a small profit, if she made a profit at all. Her trailing stop, however, got her out of the bull spread before it had much of a chance to deteriorate. The spread then proceeded to lose 300 points, and yet the trader had gotten out very near the top.

Another example of an uptrend line is seen in Figure 11.3. On the right-hand side of the coffee chart an uptrend line has been drawn connecting the May and June lows. At the time the chart was drawn the uptrend line still was intact. However, notice the two parallel lines that have been drawn around the price action connecting the December through April high and lows. This is called a *channel*. A channel is an extension of the uptrend and downtrend lines. Channels may be either upchannels or downchannels, depending on the direction they are moving. Because each high is higher than the preceding high and each low is lower than the preceding low, the coffee formation is considered an upchannel.

Channels are one of the most valuable formations a trader can find. Fortunately they occur frequently in spreads and the trader may utilize them in several ways. One possibility is to buy two units of a bull spread in an upchannel and liquidate one of them each time the price rallies to the top of the channel. The trader then buys back the liquidated unit as it drops to the bottom of the channel and then sells it if it rallies to the top of the channel again, and so on. The trader is carrying one position looking for a long-term trade. His second position is a trading unit to be bought and sold on the short-term price oscillations within the channels.

The reader may wonder why not buy the two at the bottom of the channel and sell at the top of the channel. Frequently the highs will break out of the top of the channel while the lows keep bouncing off the bottom of the channel. This would leave the trader in the untenable position of being short two units in a strong market. The trading

200 pts = $750

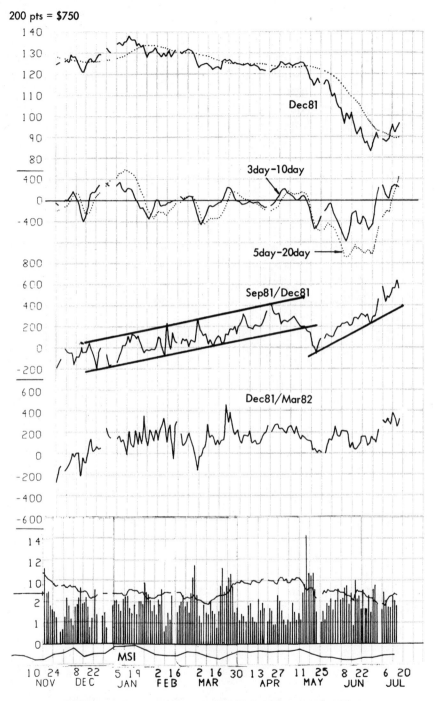

Figure 11.3   Coffee spread channel and uptrend line.

125

approach outlined above keeps the trader in for the big move that will occur over a long period of time but provide an opportunity to trade with the short-term oscillations of the markets! One look at the coffee chart shows that this strategy would have been very profitable during that time period. The March 82/March 83 GNMA chart in Figure 11.4 is a good example of why this approach is better than trying to exclusively trade the short-term moves within the channels. The March 82/March 83 GNMA spread had locked itself into a very definite downchannel. The astute trader would have been bear spreading this spread. Perhaps he was holding one bear spread for the long run and trading the short-run oscillations with the other. Following this strategy, when prices broke down through the bottom of the downtrend, accelerating their decline, the trader would have been guaranteed of having at least one bear spread still being held. The "two-way" method of trading each oscillation would have left the trader with no open positions and a small loss. He would have been trying to be long just as prices were accelerating downward.

The October feeder cattle/October live cattle chart in Figure 11.5 shows another well-formed downchannel. This one would have provided the alert trader with many opportunities as the spread moved close to the top of the downchannel on at least nine occasions.

The chart of the reverse soybean crush in Figure 11.6 shows another very definite downchannel with multiple opportunities.

One theory is that channels occur because of a slow but steady change in the fundamentals. If a theoretical value could be given to the reverse soybean crush shown, it would probably be a line drawn through the middle of the channel. The market, however, is unable to find the exact underlying value of the spread. The market tends to overshoot the value on both the upside and downside. These oscillations move it back and forth around the estimated true value at that particular moment. When the price finally breaks out of the channel, the fundamentals have probably been altered enough to move the estimated value of the spread away from the center point of the channel.

The two charts at the bottom of Figure 11.7 show some of the common channels and trend lines that can be seen in any chart. The bottom chart, September lumber versus two September plywood, shows a downtrend line which eventually gets broken in April, setting up a

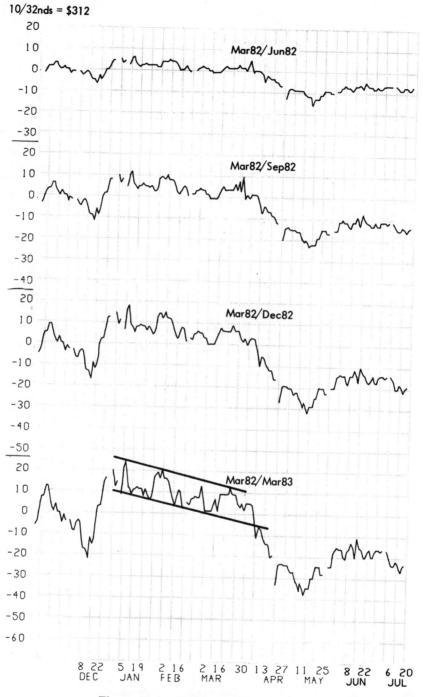

10/32nds = $312

Figure 11.4   GNMA spread channel.

127

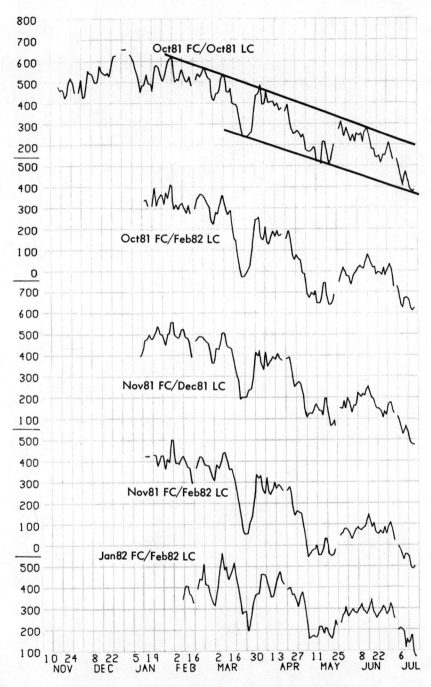

Figure 11.5 Feeder cattle/live cattle spread channel.

128

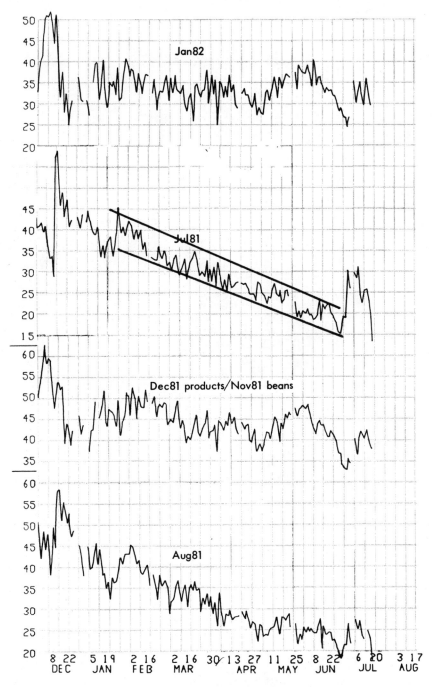

Figure 11.6   Reverse soybean crush spread channel.

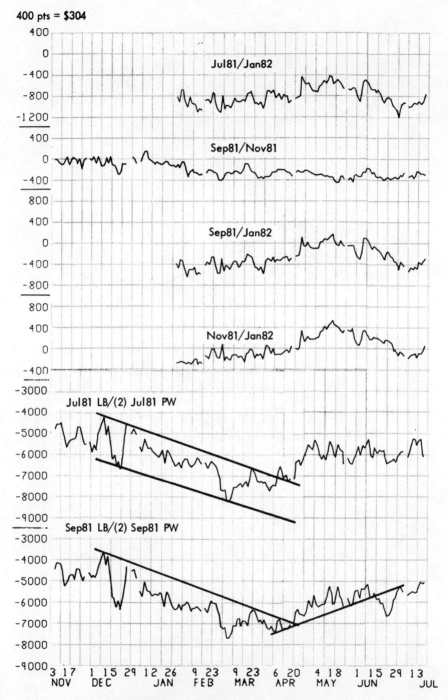

400 pts = $304

Figure 11.7   Lumber/plywood spreads.

new uptrend line which gets broken in June. This is not an uncommon occurrence and every trader should be alert to the formation and breaking of trend lines.

This chart also brings out a less common but interesting occurrence. Notice in the chart of the July lumber versus two July plywood that when the price breaks up through the downtrend line it rallies up and then comes back down and touches the downtrend line before taking off to a new or higher plateau. This move back to touch the trend line occurs with enough frequency to make it worthwhile for the spread trader to keep alert to it. It is particularly useful for the trader who has missed the breakout and wants to find a point to enter. This retracement back to the trend line can often provide this entry point.

After enough experience, the spread trader will begin to see whole series of channels and trend lines appearing on the charts. The September 81 Yen versus September 81 Swiss Franc spread in Figure 11.8 shows this clearly. A series of three channels has been outlined on the chart. However, the three channels on this chart may have been of too short a length to be useful. We can see here that as the trader has a definite channel drawn it is broken and a new one develops. Nonetheless, the trader must persevere in his chart doodlings, as occasions will occur when the trader has ample opportunities to enter profitable trades.

Some channels can be horizontal. It is in effect a trading range. The October 81 meal versus October 81 oil spread in Figure 11.9 is a good example of this. Each high goes to approximately the same point as previous highs and each low goes to approximately the same point as previous lows.

There are two ways to use this formation. One is to buy the dips to the bottom of the channel and sell rallies to the top of it. The second alternative is to initiate a spread when the price has broken up or down out of the channel. For instance, should the October 81 meal/October 81 oil spread price move down to $6,000, the trader would sell the oil and buy the meal looking for the price of the spread to continue downward. Classical technical analysis would say to place a liquidation order at the opposite side of the channel from the breakout. In our example, the top of the channel is at about $8,800 and the stop would be placed above that point. In this situation, the trader would have to put a stop valued at about $2,800 behind his position. It can be seen that a wide trading range may have a stop placed too

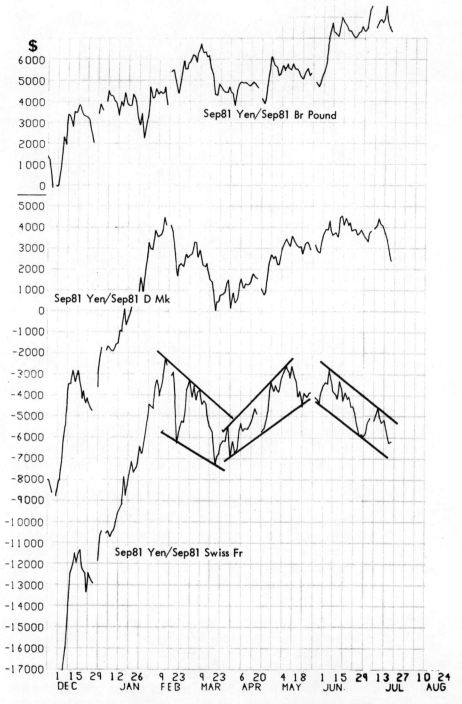

Figure 11.8   Japanese yen/Swiss franc spread channels.

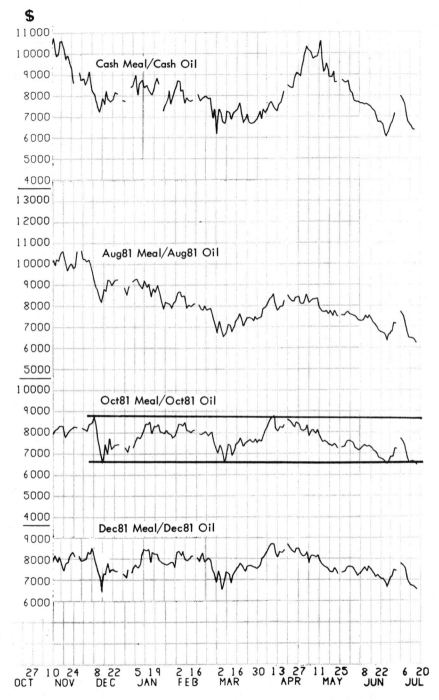

Figure 11.9   Soybean meal/soybean oil spread channel.

133

far away to be practical for the smaller trader. In this case, money management stops would be more appropriate.

The longer that prices remain within a channel, the greater the movement will be once it breaks out. The typical breakout will be sudden and dramatic. Long-term trading ranges, such as the meal/oil spread example, are relatively rare.

Spreads will often trade within a small trading range, break through one side of it, and move quickly up to a new plateau. They then form a new trading range where the process repeats itself. The July 81 Kansas City versus July 81 Chicago wheat spread in Figure 11.10 shows this kind of price behavior clearly. Prices were locked in a narrow trading range from November through January. Prices broke up through the top of the trading range and within a week had moved up into a new consolidation area where they stayed throughout most of February. A new price breakout occurred, moving the price up to a new plateau where it stayed through March and April. The final breakout occurred causing prices to move to new highs. A channel such as this shows a constant tug of war between the bulls and the bears over the spread. In the KC wheat example, the bulls were able to periodically break the hold of the bears and move prices to successively higher levels. However, the bears did not give up without a fight.

Another frequent occurrence in spreads is that a breakout into a new trading range may have, as one of its boundaries, a boundary of the previous trading range. This sounds confusing but a chart will make it clear. The December/March 82 wheat spread in Figure 11.11 shows this situation. Prices had traded in a trading range from the end of January through the end of April when they broke down through the bottom of the range. The bottom of the previous range became the top of the new range. Thus the previous support became the new resistance. Another example is in Figure 11.12 with the July/December soybean oil spread. Once again, the supporting area of the first trading range became the resistance for the second trading range.

By far the most common formation is the simple support or resistance lines. A support line is a horizontal line through at least one bottom. A resistance line goes through a top. Given such a line, the potential exists for that point to provide support or resistance should prices ever return to that level. The trading ranges were bounded on the top by resistance and the bottom by support. Notice the December 81 wheat/December 81 corn chart in Figure 11.13. Many peaks

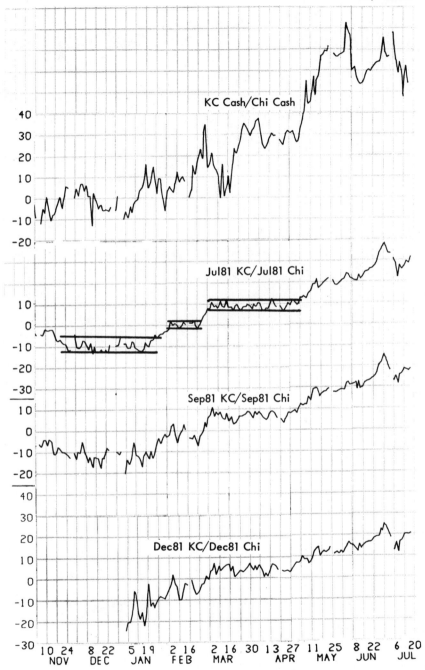

10¢ = $500

Figure 11.10 Kansas City wheat/Chicago wheat spread channels.

135

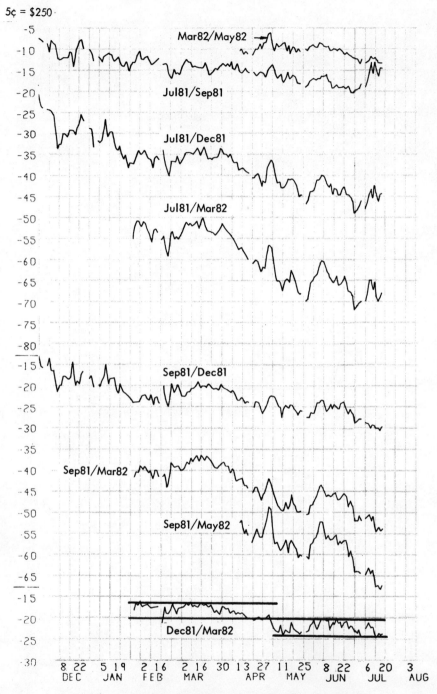

5¢ = $250

Figure 11.11   December/March wheat spread.

136

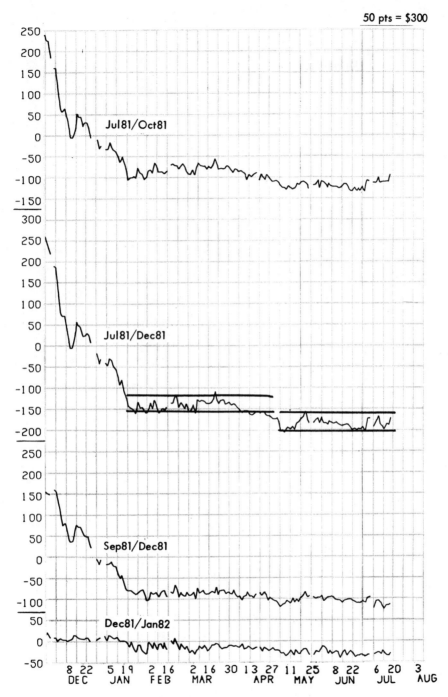

Figure 11.12   July/December soybean oil spread.

137

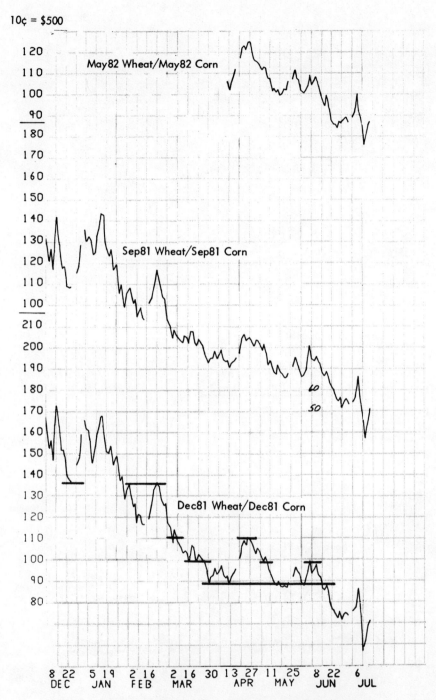

10¢ = $500

Figure 11.13   Wheat/corn spread support and resistance.

138

or troughs can become support or resistance. In fact, a support line can become a resistance line and vice versa just as was the case when prices moved out of one trading range and into another trading range. The wheat/corn chart shows a number of examples of this occurrence. Notice the number of times that the level of support became resistance if prices moved below the previous support point. The reverse can be said of the resistance levels, although our example is obviously moving in a downward direction. Traders should note the heavy support which existed at about 88 cents premium the wheat. This level was able to stop a number of price declines. Prices finally broke down through the support in the middle of June and immediately dropped almost 20 cents without stopping. Notice how the subsequent rally was unable to penetrate the previous support.

The chart in Figure 11.14 in the August 81 feeder cattle versus December 81 live cattle spread is another example of the strength of resistance and support. The bears were in firm control over this spread for the eight months shown on the graph. They were able to push the price lower in successive steps. The bulls would try to rally the price but would be stopped by heavy resistance. Two particularly potent resistance areas are shown on the graph. These resistance points would have allowed the bear spreader many opportunities to sell the spread on rallies.

The final example of support and resistance is found in Figure 11.15 in the September 81/March 82 corn spread. The same principles of support and resistance outlined above can be seen easily in this chart. In fact, it would be instructive for the trader to examine all of the charts in this group as there are numerous examples of areas where support has turned into resistance. Several other formations are also shown. The September 81/December 81 corn spread is in a well-formed downchannel.

A more interesting case is the July 81/December 81 corn spread. Notice the downtrend line formed by the November and early January highs. It was a well-formed downtrend until broken in the first part of March. This is an example of a false breakout. Unfortunately, the trader has no way of knowing it is a false breakout until after it has moved back underneath the downtrend line.

This shows one of the hazards of spread chart analysis. It is quite possible that the spread actually never traded at the point shown on the chart but that the closing prices were temporarily out of line.

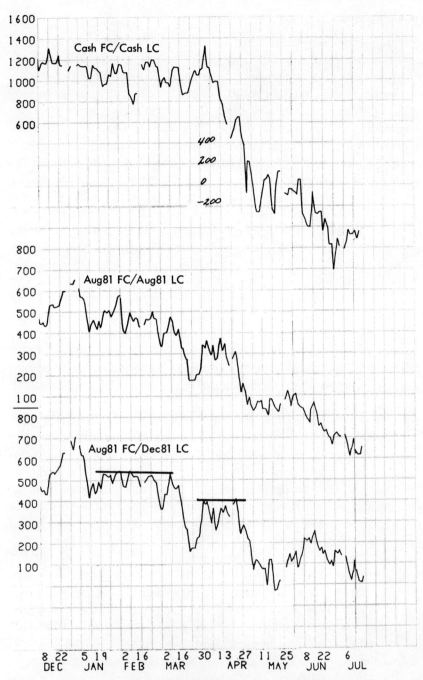

Figure 11.14   Feeder cattle/live cattle spread.

140

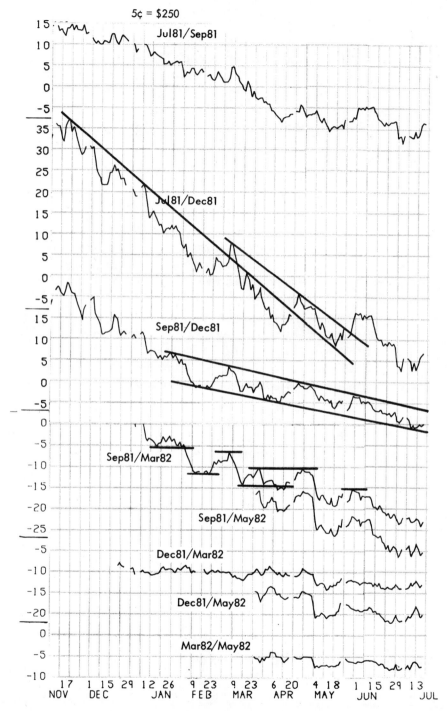

Figure 11.15   September/March corn spread.

141

Nonetheless, it can be seen that that high and the high in late April form another downtrend line which could have been used by the trader. Most chart analysis is the formation and reformation of a fairly limited selection of formations. This chart shows both the strong points and the weak points of the chart analysis. Chart analysis would have gotten the trader short the spread quite early and, with the exception of the false breakout in early March, would have kept him short for a good 40-cent move.

Another formation the trader should be alert for is the triangle. This is a formation which, for example, has all of its highs bouncing off a set support line while the lows become progressively higher. The reverse also occurs where strong support limits the declines but the highs get progressively lower. The former formation is called an ascending triangle while the latter is called a descending triangle. In the symmetrical triangle the highs are getting lower and the lows are getting higher. Let's look at some examples of triangles.

The first example is an ascending triangle. The December 81/May 82 cotton spread in Figure 11.16 shows an ascending triangle which was finally broken on the downside. This shows the major method of using triangles. They are used mainly as a means of initiating positions on breakouts either above or below the triangle.

An example of a descending triangle is the September 81/September 82 gold spread in Figure 11.17. Notice how the highs are getting lower but that support exists just below −9000. In this case, the spread broke through the upper resistance formed by the declining top of the triangle and proceeded to move into higher ground. Triangles are common in commodity spreads and should be in the repertoire of every serious commodity trader.

Sometimes the triangles may have an acute angle and at other times they can be quite fat. The Ginnie Mae spread in Figure 11.18 is an example of a very long-term shallow descending triangle. Traders should note that this particular spread broke down through support at −10, dropped 10 ticks, and then moved into a line formation.

The October 81/April 82 live cattle spread in Figure 11.19 is an example of what is usually termed a symmetrical triangle, though in this case it is not particularly symmetrical. It does, however, fit the definition of a symmetrical triangle in that the highs are getting lower and the lows are getting higher. A triangle formation of this type shows that the bulls are getting stronger on the downside and that the

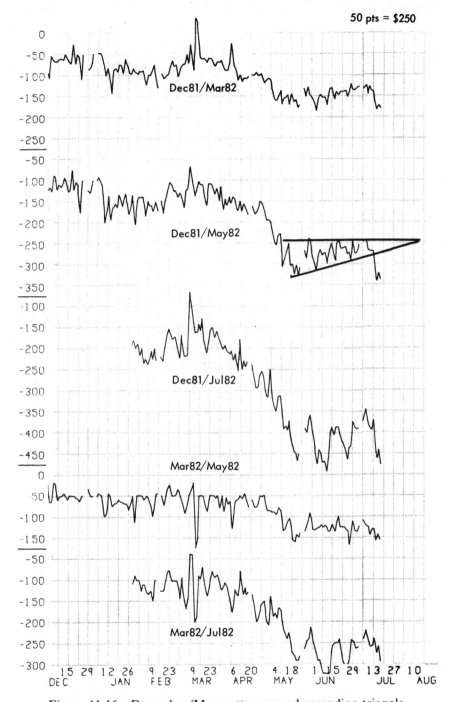

50 pts = $250

Dec81/Mar82

Dec81/May82

Dec81/Jul82

Mar82/May82

Mar82/Jul82

15 29   12 26   9 23   9 23   6 20   4. 18   1 5 29   13 27   10
DEC   JAN   FEB   MAR   APR   MAY   JUN   JUL   AUG

Figure 11.16   December/May cotton spread ascending triangle.

143

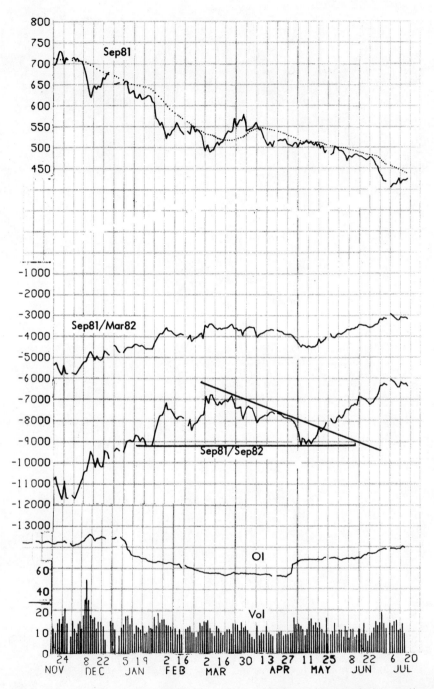

Figure 11.17   September 1981/September 1982 gold spread descending triangle.

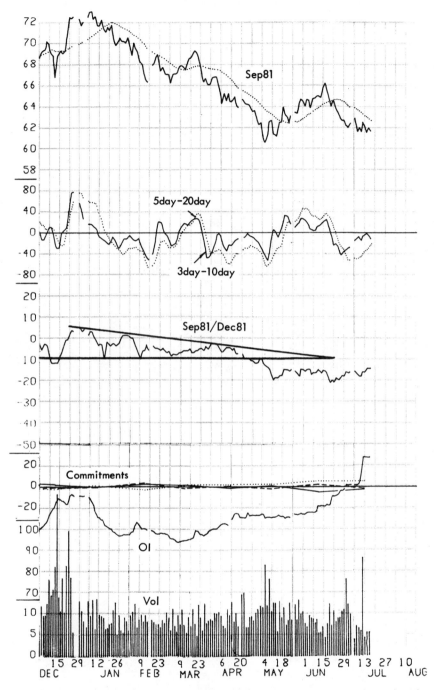

Figure 11.18   September/December GNMA spread descending triangle.

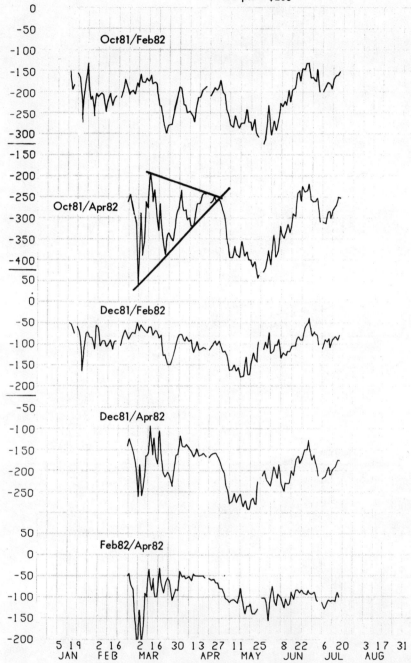

50 pts = $200

Figure 11.19   October/April cattle spread triangle.

146

bears are getting stronger on the upside. This tug-of-war must eventually give way in favor of one or the other of the two camps. Prices will then move above or below their previous highs or lows into new territory.

There are other formations found in spread charts. We have shown the formations which occur most frequently. The remaining formations are more likely to occur in outright trading than in spread trading. For example, the lumber spread of September 81/November 81 in Figure 11.20 is an example of a rounded bottom. Notice, however, that there are no other rounded bottoms in any of the other charts on the page, with the possible exception of the same time period of the July 81/November 81 spread. The reader is invited to look over the previous charts to see if there are other rounded bottoms. This tends to be a relatively rare pattern in spreads.

Double and triple bottoms occur with a high degree of frequency in spread trading. The problem is that they are usually over by the time the trader has discovered them. They are easy to see in hindsight, but they do not give the trader much opportunity to use them as a trading tool. The December 81/June 82 Treasury bond spread in Figure 11.21 shows an example of a double bottom occurring in early May. It's true that it is easy to see now that it is over, but by the time the rally was in progress, it would have been very difficult to get long the spread and find much of a profit potential left. The trader should be alert to double and triple bottoms but should not count on them being useful. They're certainly not as useful as they are in outright positions.

Other formations, such as head and shoulders and gaps and islands, either do not occur or occur with such low frequency that they are not worth looking for. A head and shoulders is an example of a formation that may not be found for many many months. Gaps do not exist as spread charts are charts connecting the closing prices. Traders thus have no way of knowing whether actual trades gapped above or below the last trade on the previous day. It would not be surprising that in some commodities gaps would be occurring all the time due to the low volume of actual spread trading. Since this is the case, gaps would have limited usefulness.

Traders should try to use the technical formations outlined as methods of initiating and liquidating trades. All formations show lines of support and resistance. The support may be level as in the bottom of

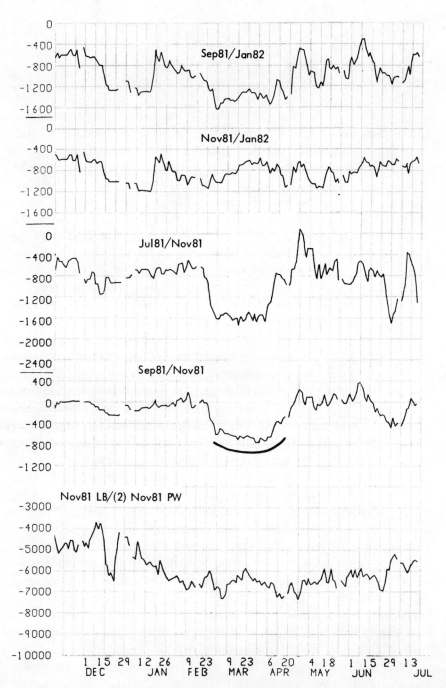

Figure 11.20 September/November lumber spread rounded bottom.

148

10/32nds = $312

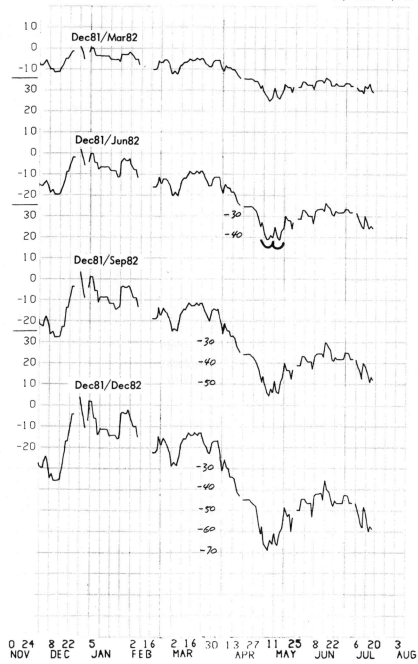

Figure 11.21   December/June Treasury Bond spread double bottom.

a trading range or in a simple support area or it may be increasing as in an uptrend line, an upchannel, or an ascending triangle. The support may be declining support as in the case of a downchannel.

The basic rule is to buy spreads just above support with liquidation points just underneath the support. Traders should sell spreads just under resistance with liquidation points just above resistance. Aggressive traders may reverse positions as the spread hits the liquidation points. The December 82 T-bond versus December 82 Ginnie Mae spread in Figure 11.22 has been marked to show initiation and stop points. After the ascending triangle has been formed by the highs and lows in December, January, and February, the aggressive trader would have initiated bull spreads whenever the price moved close to the ascending support line with a stop just below it. The aggressive trader would have sold the spread whenever prices reached the support line, placing stops just above the support. It can be seen in the chart that a total of five spreads would have been initiated with only the last one having actually been stopped out. This point is marked with an SR, designating a stop reversal. This triangle formation shows that initiation can take place with a slanting support or resistance as well as a horizontal support or resistance line.

To carry this example a step further, suppose that the trader, for other reasons, felt that the December 82 T-bond was going to gain on the December 82 Ginnie Mae. He thus does not want to play it from the short side. He would then initiate positions only when the price moved down to the ascending support line. He could consider the upward trend to be intact until the price had broken below it. In this particular example he would treat the trading as if it were an uptrend rather than as an ascending triangle. Alternatively, he could use the two-unit technique. He would buy two units at the beginning of March, liquidating one on the rally top in the middle of March. He would buy back the second unit when prices dipped again early in May. He would liquidate the second unit on the one-week rally subsequent to the purchase, but would replace the unit as the price breaks up through the resistance line. In this case the stop reversal is not so much a stop but a new initiation. Had the price moved below the uptrend line he probably would have liquidated both positions and stood aside from the marketplace. He would do this because he had other reasons for believing that the price would continue in an uptrend. If he had reversed when prices moved below the uptrend

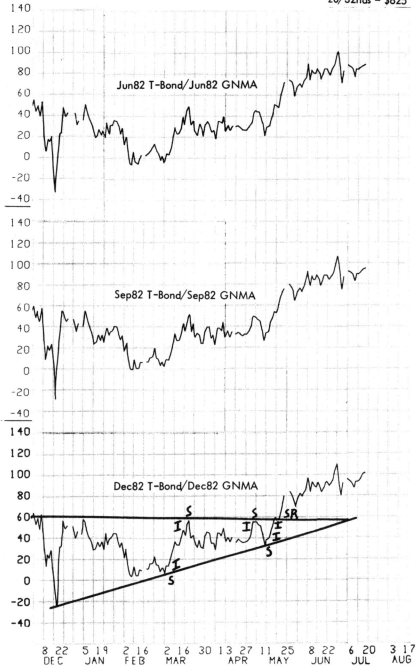

20/32nds = $625

Figure 11.22   Treasury Bond/GNMA spread trading.

line, he would be fighting against his rationale for being in the trade.

Suppose that the trader, after being long the T-bond and short the Ginnie Mae for some time, came to believe that conditions had changed and that a downward move in the spread was going to occur. In this situation, he would place a reversal stop below the support rather than a simple stop. (Let me reiterate that there are no spread stop orders but that we are using the word stop in the sense of liquidating the trade.)

Technical chart analysis can be a powerful trading tool in and of itself. Many traders trade spreads purely from technical grounds. The author occasionally does this, particularly in a breakout of a trading range. Other spread traders prefer to use technical analysis to give them a point to place initiation and liquidation orders. No matter how the trader uses technical analysis, he must pay attention to it or risk being taken out of an otherwise profitable position due to short-run technical factors.

TWELVE

Intermarket Spreads

Several commodities are traded on more than one market. For example, wheat is traded on three separate markets—the Chicago Board of Trade, the Kansas City Board of Trade, and the Minneapolis Grain Exchange. Silver is traded on the Chicago Board of Trade, the Commodity Exchange in New York, and the London Metal Exchange. Coffee is traded in New York and London. Gold is traded in Chicago and New York.

Intermarket spreads entail the purchase of a contract in one market and the sale of another in the other market. For instance, a trader could buy Chicago wheat and sell Kansas City wheat. Intermarket spreads are relatively hard to initiate because they take place in different markets, cities, or even continents. Brokers accept them as basically two outright positions. When a trader gives an intermarket spread order to a broker on a limit basis the broker may execute it, usually on a "not held" basis. In other words, the broker will try but won't guarantee that the prices will be within the limit.

Intermarket spreads generally are regarded as the most complicated spreads. The necessity of analyzing two markets and the fine distinctions between contract specifications is sometimes too complicated for the novice commodity trader. Intermarket spreads are usually left until some degree of confidence and competence has been built up by trading other types of spreads.

153

PROFITING ON CURRENCY FLUCTUATIONS

Before the advent of foreign currency futures on the International Monetary Market, intermarket spreads between United States and London silver were a popular way of speculating on the price of the British pound. It may seem somewhat odd to be able to speculate on the value of the British pound by trading silver in two different markets. Nonetheless, it was a very popular occupation of many traders. Silver was perhaps the most popular trading vehicle, but cocoa, coffee, and sugar all had their adherents.

Suppose that silver was selling for $10.00 per ounce in the United States at the same time that the British pound was worth $2.00. Simple arithmetic shows that 1 ounce of silver would then be worth £5.00 in British currency. Should the British pound remain at $2.00, the price of silver in London and New York would rise and fall each day the same amount after converting the currency into its counterpart. The price could be converted into either currency and would be the same.

Actually, the price could vary slightly, though there are limits as to how far the price can change from one market to another. Silver, whether it is traded in London or New York or Chicago, is the same commodity. There are no contract specification differences that are worth talking about. If the price in one market were to gain by a large amount on the other market, speculators would take delivery on contracts in the first market and deliver them against the contract in the second market. This constant threat of delivery in one market and redelivery in another market keeps the prices of the two markets' commodities within a very narrow limit. The maximum that one commodity in one market can be above or below the value of the same commodity in another market is the value of the transaction costs, such as commissions, and the transportation to the new market. It is within this band of transportation and transaction costs that the price will oscillate. For purposes of our example, let us assume that prices do not vary within the transportation and transaction cost band. Let us assume that a change in price causes an identical move in the other market due to the effects of the arbitrageurs. Although this will not be entirely accurate, it will simplify the example. The oscillations within the transaction and transportation band tend to be minor anyway.

The main point behind intermarket spreads where the two markets are priced in different currencies is that a change in price in one market will be the same price in the other market after the currencies have been converted. If the price of silver is $10.00 an ounce in New York, it will be £5.00 per ounce in London if the British pound is worth $2.00. If the price of silver rises to $11.00 an ounce in New York, it will sell for £5.50 in London. Conversely, should the price of silver drop to £4.00 per ounce in London, the trader will know that it will be selling for $8.00 per ounce in New York. This principle of equality occurs whether the commodity is silver, coffee, cocoa, sugar, or whatever.

This principle completely breaks down should the value of the British pound change in relation to the U.S. dollar. If the British pound changes value, then the value of the commodity must also change to take into account the new value of the pound.

To convert the price of a commodity from one currency to another, one merely divides the price of the commodity in one currency by the price of the other currency in terms of the first currency. Thus silver at $10.00 an ounce divided by $2.00 per pound equals £5.00. If the price of the British pound were to move to $2.20, the price of silver in London would move to £4.55 per ounce. The price of silver in London would have dropped 10% even though it was stable in New York. Conversely, if the value of the British pound had dropped to $1.65, the price of silver in London would be £6.06 per ounce. Once again, the price of silver has remained steady at $10.00 per ounce in New York but its price has moved dramatically in British pounds.

Every morning, when the exchanges open in New York, the opening price is usually a function of how London closed and the change in currency values. As can be seen, it is quite possible that the commodity value did not change but that the currency value did, thus necessitating a change in the New York opening price. There are also occasions when the price change in London will be offset largely by currency changes. It should also be noted that the London opening price is also a function of the previous New York close and the currency changes.

Let's assume that a trader is bearish on the British pound. To profit from the expected movement, he could buy London silver and sell New York silver. To continue our above example, let us assume that New York silver is at $10.00, London silver is at £5.00, and hence the British pound is worth $2.00.

Let's take a look at in tabular form what would happen should the price of silver in U.S. dollars remain the same and the British pound drop in value to $1.50:

Initiate

British pound = $2.00

N.Y. silver = $10.00

London silver = £5.00

Sell N.Y. silver and buy London silver

Liquidate

British pound = $1.50

N.Y. silver = $10.00

London silver = £6.67

Sell London silver and buy N.Y. silver

Effects

The trader has the same number of U.S. dollars but now has £1.67 more than at the beginning of the transaction. £1.67 is worth $2.50 after conversion at the new exchange rate.

The amount of profit on the transaction does not depend on the change of the price of silver. In the example above, the trader was able to pick up a profit of £1.67 on the decline of the British pound when silver stayed at $10.00. Let's take a look at this transaction if silver had fallen to $5.00 an ounce.

Initiate

British pound = $2.00

N.Y. silver = $10.00

London silver = £5.00
Sell N.Y. silver and buy London silver

Liquidate

British pound = $1.50
N.Y. silver = $5.00
London silver = £3.33
Buy N.Y. silver and sell London silver

Effect

The trader now has an additional $5.00 but has £1.67 less. His net is plus $2.50. His loss of £1.67, worth $2.50 after converting, must be subtracted from his gain of $5.00 from the sale of the N.Y. silver.

Notice that the two transactions have the same profit even though the price of silver was substantially different in the two examples. The profit to the trader came about solely through the change in the price of the British pound. The price of silver does not affect the trader's profit because the two silver positions offset each other.

The same principles of currency change apply whether the commodity is silver or another commodity that is denominated in two different currencies. Figure 12.1 is a matrix which shows the value of London silver in pence at various values of silver and the British pound.

It is recommended that traders wishing to use international spreads as currency speculation vehicles stick to silver. There are slight differences in the contracts of the other commodities which may distort relationships from the currency and commodity value. For example, the most frequently traded coffee contract in New York is for South American styles of coffee. The British contract calls for delivery of Robusta coffee. Thus a change in value may occur simply because of the relative supply and demand changes between the two types of coffee rather than between the currency values.

Also, traders should remember that the British pound contract is very liquid and successful on the International Monetary Market. This could provide an alternative to trading intermarket silver spreads.

BRITISH POUND PRICES

SILVER PRICES	1.00	1.20	1.40	1.60	1.80	2.00	2.20	2.40	2.60	2.80	3.00
4.00	4.00	3.33	2.86	2.50	2.22	2.00	1.82	1.67	1.54	1.43	1.33
5.00	5.00	4.17	3.57	3.13	2.78	2.50	2.27	2.08	1.92	1.79	1.67
6.00	6.00	5.00	4.29	3.75	3.33	3.00	2.73	2.50	2.31	2.14	2.00
7.00	7.00	5.83	5.00	4.38	3.89	3.50	3.18	2.92	2.69	2.50	2.33
8.00	8.00	6.67	5.71	5.00	4.44	4.00	3.64	3.33	3.08	2.86	2.67
9.00	9.00	7.50	6.43	5.63	5.00	4.50	4.09	3.75	3.46	3.21	3.00
10.00	10.00	8.33	7.14	6.25	5.56	5.00	4.55	4.17	3.85	3.57	3.33
11.00	11.00	9.17	7.86	6.88	6.11	5.50	5.00	4.58	4.23	3.93	3.67
12.00	12.00	10.00	8.57	7.50	6.67	6.00	5.45	5.00	4.62	4.29	4.00
13.00	13.00	10.83	9.29	8.13	7.22	6.50	5.91	5.42	5.00	4.64	4.33
14.00	14.00	11.67	10.00	8.75	7.78	7.00	6.36	5.83	5.38	5.00	4.67
15.00	15.00	12.50	10.71	9.38	8.33	7.50	6.82	6.25	5.77	5.36	5.00
16.00	16.00	13.33	11.43	10.00	8.89	8.00	7.27	6.67	6.15	5.71	5.33
17.00	17.00	14.17	12.14	10.63	9.44	8.50	7.73	7.08	6.54	6.07	5.67
18.00	18.00	15.00	12.86	11.25	10.00	9.00	8.18	7.50	6.92	6.43	6.00
19.00	19.00	15.83	13.57	11.88	10.56	9.50	8.64	7.92	7.31	6.79	6.33
20.00	20.00	16.67	14.29	12.50	11.11	10.00	9.09	8.33	7.69	7.14	6.67

Figure 12.1   Price of silver at various values of the British Pound.

158

Transaction costs would be lower as only one commission need be paid. The trader would not have to pay a full commission in New York and a full commission in London.

The main advantage of using the intermarket silver spread is that it can provide lower volatility than the British pound futures. The lower volatility may allow the trader to control risk better and feel more comfortable in his position.

Before initiating an intermarket silver spread with one leg in London, the trader should check with a broker on margin requirements. Typically, the trader must put up margin for both sides of the transaction.

SHORT SQUEEZE ARBITRAGES

It is rare that anybody but a floor trader can pull off an arbitrage transaction. As you will recall, arbitrage is basically the buying of the contract in one market coupled with the simultaneous selling in a different market. It usually takes place within the transportation/transaction price band. The floor trader, with virtually nonexistent brokerage costs, is able to arbitrage profitably while the average speculator is usually prohibited from participating in arbitrage because of the high commission costs. Only rarely will prices get out of line enough to permit arbitrage transactions to be executed by the average speculator.

This typically occurs whenever there is some type of panic buying or selling, possibly in a short squeeze situation. This has occasionally given speculators the opportunity to buy contracts in one market and sell them in the other market and be able to take a small profit. These situations rarely last more than a couple of days. The speculator must therefore be not only alert but also quick.

This situation has occurred a few times in the silver market. The trader has, in effect, been able to arbitrage between the Chicago and New York silver markets. It has usually happened when there was a large movement of silver stocks from deliverable positions for one exchange to deliverable positions for the other exchange. Because, in the past, silver open interest has remained very large up until first notice day, the threat of a short squeeze has had a big impact on expiring months. However, the threat may occur in one market but not in the other. It is thus possible that the different expiring contracts in the two different markets may be trading 3 to 5 cents apart. This type of difference can provide a profit opportunity for the spreader who is willing to take delivery in one month in one contract and deliver it against the contract in the other market. Silver is relatively easy to do this in as the commodity has low transportation costs. Nonetheless, before embarking on ths type of project, the speculator must discover the terms of the delivery conditions in both markets as well as the transaction and transportation costs. Also, the spread trader should not wait patiently for this type of opportunity to occur.

INTERMARKET WHEAT SPREADS

The most common type of intermarket spreads are the wheat spreads between the Chicago Board of Trade, the Kansas City Board of Trade, and the Minneapolis Grain Exchange. This happens in large volume every day as traders try to profit from the changes in the supply and demand between the three different exchanges.

There are three types of wheat traded on commodity exchanges in the United States. Hard red winter wheat is traded at the Kansas City Board of Trade. Northern spring wheat is the type of wheat traded at the Minneapolis Grain Exchange. Theoretically, hard red winter, northern spring, and soft red winter wheat can all be delivered at the Chicago Board of Trade. As a practical matter, trading focuses on the supply and demand for soft red winter wheat. This is because the three exchanges concentrate on the type of wheat grown in their immediate areas. Soft red winter wheat is the type of wheat grown nearest Chicago, but the exchange allows the delivery of the other two types of wheat against their wheat contract. The other two exchanges allow the delivery of one type of wheat only.

Traders should note that the three types of wheat tend to have different uses. The hard red wheat is used for bread while the soft red wheat is usually used for crackers. All three types of wheat are, to a limited extent, interchangeable. This means that the prices of the various types of wheat cannot be too different from one another. If the price of one variety of wheat gains too much on another variety of wheat, wheat users will change the blend of wheat in their processing to make more use of the more inexpensive wheat.

Another factor which tends to keep the price of the wheats related is the ability to deliver any type of wheat against the Chicago contract. If the price of the futures contract in Chicago, which is mainly based on the fundamentals of soft red wheat, were to gain dramatically enough on the Kansas City contract, wheat owners might find it to their advantage to barge hard red wheat from Kansas City to Chicago and deliver it against the contract there. The net effect of this is to limit the amount that Chicago futures can rise above Kansas City and Minneapolis futures by approximately the cost of purchasing and shipping the wheat from Kansas City or Minneapolis to Chicago. It is possible, however, for the Chicago contract to rise above these costs for a short time. If the price of the Chicago contract moves high enough to induce people to move wheat from outlying areas to Chicago, the price may stay high during the time it takes for the outlying wheat to be loaded and shipped to Chicago. Also, it will most likely take more than one bargeload of wheat to change the fundamental picture in Chicago enough to bring it in line with Kansas City and Minneapolis. The net effect is that prices will rarely go above the point that will bring wheat into Chicago from other points but, once it happens, there may be a time lag before it moves back below that point.

This more or less limiting factor can be compared with the concept of carrying charges. The price can move to a certain point but is unlikely to go beyond it. The trader can thereby profit by putting on short Chicago and long Kansas City or Minneapolis spreads when prices reach the point where wheat will be shipped into Chicago. The trader should contact a broker to find out the costs to ship wheat from the various markets into Chicago. These costs change and the trader should be alert for this as it could affect the trade.

It is important to note that the Chicago market is the only market that allows the delivery of more than one variety of wheat. This means that the Kansas City and Minneapolis contract prices can go above the Chicago price added to the costs of moving the wheat to those markets.

The three wheat markets, however, rarely get to a point where barge rates come into play. Only a large relative shortage of soft red wheat could cause intermarket deliveries to become a market factor.

The spreads between the three markets mainly respond to the relative supply and demand between the markets.

One major factor is the different growing seasons. The two winter wheats, traded in Kansas City and Chicago, are harvested in May, June, and July. The first new crop contract is the July contract and the last old crop contract is the May contract. The spring wheat, traded on the Minneapolis exchange, is harvested in late summer. The first new crop contract is the September contract and the last old crop contract is the July contract.

This creates a number of seasonal trades. The July contracts in Kansas City and Chicago will tend to lose to the July Minneapolis contract because they will be burdened with large new crop supplies while the Minneapolis will be scraping the bottom of the old crop barrel. The Minneapolis September contract will tend to lose the Chicago and Kansas City September contracts for much the same reason but to a lesser degree. The Kansas City and Chicago contracts will be starting a seasonal rise in price while the Minneapolis contract will be dropping due to the increasing supplies of harvest.

The market focuses mainly on the size of the new crops and total supplies to find the relative value between the various new crop contracts. This is particularly true with the two winter wheat contracts because they are harvested at similar times. Traders can use the techniques discussed in Chapter 10 on regression and correlation analysis to obtain the implied values in various combinations of productions and supplies between the markets.

The same methods are valuable when analyzing the last old crop contract for each wheat. The market concentrates on the old crop carryout figure and, to a lesser extent, on new crop prospects when trading the May contracts for Kansas City and Chicago and the July contract for Minneapolis. The trader should examine ratios of carryouts of the various wheats to help him decide which wheat should be priced higher and by how much.

For intermarket spreads between months not at the beginning or end of a crop year, the trader should examine deliverable stocks and demand prospects. In the final analysis, futures contracts are contracts on the deliverable supplies of a commodity. When push comes to shove, the supply and demand for a commodity futures contract is the supply and demand for the deliverable supplies. The intermarket wheat trader should examine closely the deliverable stocks figure released weekly by the exchanges to obtain clues to the relative supply and demand and hence price differences between the different wheat. If one wheat has very low deliverable stocks compared to another wheat, its price will gain on the second wheat.

The trader can get an idea of the coming weeks' deliverable stocks figure by keeping track of the daily receipts and shipments figures. This information is issued daily over wire services and can be gotten from a knowledgeable broker. Also, deliverable stocks show a seasonal increase and decline. The biggest time of increase is immediately following harvest. Stocks slowly work their way down for the rest of the season.

Demand prospects also influence the intermarket wheat spreads. A large demand for a particular type of wheat will usually lead to a decline in deliverable stocks and tighten the supply/demand situation relative to another type of wheat.

It should be noted that traders do not necessarily have to trade the same contracts in the two different markets. That is to say the trader does not need to buy December Kansas City wheat and sell December Chicago wheat. The trader should be striving to find the optimal combination of contracts to buy and sell. It may be that the trader decides to sell December Chicago wheat and buy March Kansas City wheat because the fundamentals for Kansas City wheat will be more bullish in March and the most bearish fundamental will be in the December contract for Chicago.

Traders can use some of the other techniques in this book to determine which contract would be the best alternative for trading. In particular, the sections on bull and bear spreads and carrying charge spreads would be the most applicable.

Commission costs tend to be double because traders must pay full commissions on both sides of the spread. There is typically a break in margins, though. Brokerage houses will usually allow the intermarket spreader to put up the margin on the side of the spread which requires the highest margin. Thus if the Chicago wheat margin is $1,500 and Kansas City wheat takes $1,200, the spread trader would be required to put up $1,500 as a margin deposit.

THIRTEEN

Intercommodity Spreads

Many commodities have similar uses and can be substituted for one another in certain circumstances. Spreads between these types of commodities are called intercommodity spreads. As an example, corn and oats are both used for feeding animals. The prices of these two commodities can vary over a wide range but there is a limit as to how far the price of one commodity can go over the price of the other commodity. If the price of corn were to gain too much on the price of oats, animal feeders would stop using the corn and substitute oats. This substitution would depress the price of corn while increasing the price of oats. Thus the price relationship between the two commodities would be forced back into line.

The commodities are usually related to each other in that they are substitutes for each other. Thus wheat versus corn, corn versus oats, hogs versus cattle, and Treasury bonds versus GNMAs would all be examples of popular intercommodity spreads.

Another popular intercommodity spread relationship is that of a commodity and its products. Probably the two most popular intercommodity spreads of this type are the soybean versus soybean meal and soybean oil spread and the hog versus bellies spread. These are commodities which are related by one side of the spread being a product of the other side of the spread.

165

A third type of intercommodity spread is the soybean meal versus soybean oil spread. These two commodities are not related because of substitutability but because they are both products of the same commodity—soybeans. The supply and demand for one of the commodities has a strong effect on the supply and demand for the other commodity.

All other spreads which are between two commodities do not fall into the category we have delineated as intercommodity. They may, in fact, be between two commodities but unless there is some type of relationship between the two commodities we do not call them intercommodity. Although the word "intercommodity" means between commodities, the qualifying attribute of some type of relationship has been added to narrow the field. Thus a long Mexican peso/short feeder cattle spread may be between two commodities but it is not considered an intercommodity spread.

Intercommodity spreads frequently are considered the most complicated spreads to trade. Novice traders tend to shy away from them because of the potentially complex interaction between the two commodities. They also tend to be fundamentally oriented and hence require a more complete knowledge of the underlying fundamentals of the two commodities. Traders usually learn to trade other spreads before attempting intercommodity spreads.

Perhaps the largest portion of intercommodity spreads is between the various grains. Wheat, corn, and oats can all be used as feed grains. However, the grains do not have a one-to-one relationship with each other. For instance, wheat contains roughly 15% more protein than does corn. Thus the price of wheat will typically be at least 15% more than the price of corn.

WHEAT VERSUS CORN

Wheat versus corn is one of the most popular intercommodity spreads, if not the most popular. It has several interesting features that the spread trader should be aware of. The major factors to keep in mind are the supply and demand of the two commodities and the seasonality of production. If all things were equal, wheat would sell for 15% more than corn because of the extra feed value, but things are never equal. Hence wheat will trade for a greater or lesser premium than 15%. Because wheat is used mainly as a food grain rather than a feed grain, its uses tend to be different from corn. It is this extra utility as a food grain which typically allows it to trade for greater than its feed value over the price of corn. If corn was selling for $3.00 a bushel, one would expect wheat to trade at $3.45 a bushel based on its feed value. However, because of its use in bread, crackers, pastries, and so on, its value is usually much higher than 15% above the corn price. It is not unusual to see wheat sell for $4.00 a bushel when corn is selling for $3.00 a bushel.

The major value of examining the supply and demand is to try to discover what the range will be in the spread. A year with a very large supply of wheat and a low supply of corn will have wheat selling for a much closer value to corn than if the reverse were true. In fact, in several years, where there was a large supply of wheat relative to corn, the price of wheat actually was below the price of corn. It did not sell there for a particularly long period of time but, nonetheless, it should alert traders of the possibility that the 15% greater feed value does not necessarily present a floor to the value of wheat over corn. People take time to adjust their feeding rations and wheat does have different properties as feed. The major types of wheat in the United States were developed for bread and bread products, not for feed wheat. Therefore, the animal feeders, even with the price of wheat below corn, will not turn to exclusively wheat over corn. The wheat creates a meat slightly different from the corn. What the feeders do is to introduce larger quantities of wheat to the diet, but they do not feed exclusively wheat.

One potential clue to the value of the wheat versus the corn is the ratio of their total supplies. When there is a large supply of wheat relative to corn, the demand for wheat will have to be exceptionally strong to move its price to a level much higher than corn's price.

The other major factor to consider when trading wheat versus corn is the seasonality of production. Wheat is harvested mainly in June and July while corn is harvested in October through December. The first new crop contract of wheat is July and the first new crop contract for corn is December. Both wheat and corn reach their price lows for the year typically during the harvest period. The July contract tends to be the weakest contract for corn.

Because July is a seasonally strong month for corn because of the slowly reducing supply and yet consistent demand, the price of July corn tends to gain on the price of July wheat from the period of the preceding December through to the expiration of the July contract. From that point until the following December the situation changes. December corn typically is the weakest month for corn while December is a reasonably firm wheat contract. Thus from July through to December, December wheat tends to gain on December corn. Figures 13.1 and 13.2 show the seasonality of the various contracts.

DECEMBER WHEAT

11 YEARS

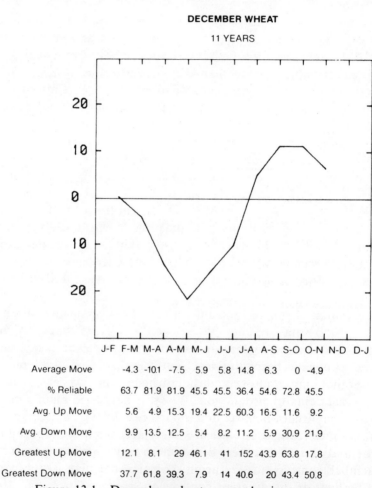

	J-F	F-M	M-A	A-M	M-J	J-J	J-A	A-S	S-O	O-N	N-D	D-J
Average Move		-4.3	-10.1	-7.5	5.9	5.8	14.8	6.3	0	-4.9		
% Reliable		63.7	81.9	81.9	45.5	45.5	36.4	54.6	72.8	45.5		
Avg. Up Move		5.6	4.9	15.3	19.4	22.5	60.3	16.5	11.6	9.2		
Avg. Down Move		9.9	13.5	12.5	5.4	8.2	11.2	5.9	30.9	21.9		
Greatest Up Move		12.1	8.1	29	46.1	41	152	43.9	63.8	17.8		
Greatest Down Move		37.7	61.8	39.3	7.9	14	40.6	20	43.4	50.8		

Figure 13.1   December wheat seasonal price pattern.

DECEMBER CORN

11 YEARS

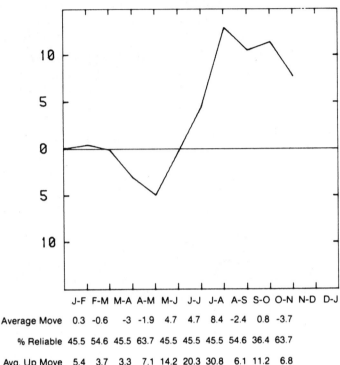

	J-F	F-M	M-A	A-M	M-J	J-J	J-A	A-S	S-O	O-N	N-D	D-J
Average Move	0.3	-0.6	-3	-1.9	4.7	4.7	8.4	-2.4	0.8	-3.7		
% Reliable	45.5	54.6	45.5	63.7	45.5	45.5	45.5	54.6	36.4	63.7		
Avg. Up Move	5.4	3.7	3.3	7.1	14.2	20.3	30.8	6.1	11.2	6.8		
Avg. Down Move	3.9	4.3	10.5	7.1	3.3	8.3	10.2	9.5	5.1	9.7		
Greatest Up Move	19.1	8.9	7.7	19.6	26	59.9	59.8	10.2	31.7	12.5		
Greatest Down Move	13.4	10.7	29	17.4	6.9	21.3	19.8	36.4	17.4	22.9		

Figure 13.2   December corn seasonal price pattern.

This spread has been a favorite of seasonal traders for many years. The specific highs and low and the exact timing are a function of the supply and demand of the two commodities for that particular year.

A similar situation exists in the corn versus oats spread. This has been another favorite as oats are harvested much the same time as wheat and thus reach their seasonal lows with either the July or September contracts. Once again, the seasonal play is very strong here because of the different production seasons. Once again, however, the supply and demand of the two commodities must be kept in mind to discover the limits of the move as well as getting some clues to short-term timing. Regression and correlation analysis can be very useful in this context.

One further consideration is that it is traditional to spread two contracts of oats for every one contract of corn. For example, the spread trader would buy 10,000 bushels of December oats and sell 5,000 bushels of December corn. This ratio of two bushels of oats to one bushel of corn is used because a bushel of oats weighs 32 pounds compared with 56 pounds for a bushel of corn.

Unlike the wheat versus corn spread, the feed value of oats is considered essentially equal to the feed value of corn on a per pound basis. Note that the feed value is considered to be equal on a per pound basis rather than on a per bushel basis. This is what provides the necessity to spread two contracts of oats for every one contract of corn.

Once again, the major factors to consider in terms of supply and demand are the total supply of each commodity and the deliverable stocks. The method of analysis is much the same as the wheat/corn with the emphasis on some type of ratio related to price as the means of analysis.

CATTLE VERSUS HOGS

Cattle versus hogs is another popular intercommodity spread. The major methods of analysis are the relative supply and demand and the seasonal factors. One small point is that it is necessary to trade three contracts of cattle versus four contracts of hogs, because a contract of cattle is for 40,000 pounds while the hog contract calls for delivery of 30,000 pounds.

The first task of the cattle versus hog spreader is to analyze the relative supply and demand for the two commodities during the periods that the trader wishes to spread. Typically most traders are trading the same months, that is, December hogs versus December cattle. This is not necessarily the optimal procedure to use at all times. Nonetheless, with that caveat in mind, the spread trader is trying to analyze the supply and demand for cattle and hogs for particular

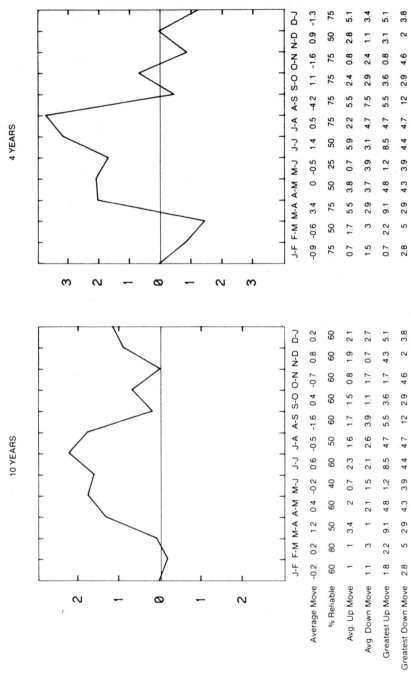

CATTLE NEAREST FUTURES

10 YEARS

CATTLE NEAREST FUTURES

4 YEARS

	J-F	F-M	M-A	A-M	M-J	J-J	J-A	A-S	S-O	O-N	N-D	D-J
Average Move	-0.2	0.2	1.2	0.4	-0.2	0.6	-0.5	-1.6	0.4	-0.7	0.8	0.2
% Reliable	60	80	50	60	40	60	50	60	60	60	60	60
Avg. Up Move	1	1	3.4	2	0.7	2.3	1.6	1.7	1.5	0.8	1.9	2.1
Avg. Down Move	1.1	3	1	2.1	1.5	2.1	2.6	3.9	1.1	1.7	0.7	2.7
Greatest Up Move	1.8	2.2	9.1	4.8	1.2	8.5	4.7	5.5	3.6	1.7	4.3	5.1
Greatest Down Move	2.8	5	2.9	4.3	3.9	4.4	4.7	12	2.9	4.6	2	3.8

	J-F	F-M	M-A	A-M	M-J	J-J	J-A	A-S	S-O	O-N	N-D	D-J
	-0.9	-0.6	3.4	0	-0.5	1.4	0.5	-4.2	1.1	-1.6	0.9	-1.3
		75	50	75	50	25	50	75	75	75	75	50	75
	0.7	1.7	5.5	3.8	0.7	5.9	2.2	5.5	2.4	0.8	2.8	5.1
	1.5	3	2.9	3.7	3.9	3.1	4.7	7.5	2.9	2.4	1.1	3.4
	0.7	2.2	9.1	4.8	1.2	8.5	4.7	5.5	3.6	0.8	3.1	5.1
	2.8	5	2.9	4.3	3.9	4.4	4.7	12	2.9	4.6	2	3.8

Figure 13.3   Nearest futures cattle seasonal price pattern.

171

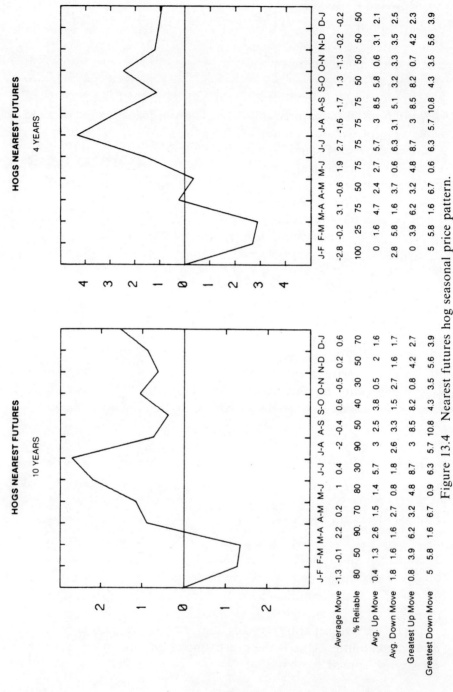

Figure 13.4 Nearest futures hog seasonal price pattern.

HOGS NEAREST FUTURES

10 YEARS

	J-F	F-M	M-A	A-M	M-J	J-J	J-A	A-S	S-O	O-N	N-D	D-J
Average Move	-1.3	-0.1	2.2	0.2	1	0.4	-2	-0.4	0.6	-0.5	0.2	0.6
% Reliable	80	50	90.	70	80	30	90	50	40	30	50	70
Avg. Up Move	0.4	1.3	2.6	1.5	1.4	5.7	3	2.5	3.8	0.5	2	1.6
Avg. Down Move	1.8	1.6	1.6	2.7	0.8	1.8	2.6	3.3	1.5	2.7	1.6	1.7
Greatest Up Move	0.8	3.9	6.2	3.2	4.8	8.7	3	8.5	8.2	0.8	4.2	2.7
Greatest Down Move	5	5.8	1.6	6.7	0.9	6.3	5.7	10.8	4.3	3.5	5.6	3.9

HOGS NEAREST FUTURES

4 YEARS

	J-F	F-M	M-A	A-M	M-J	J-J	J-A	A-S	S-O	O-N	N-D	D-J
Average Move	-2.8	-0.2	3.1	-0.6	1.9	2.7	-1.6	-1.7	1.3	-1.3	-0.2	-0.2
% Reliable	100	25	75	50	75	75	75	75	50	50	50	50
Avg. Up Move	0	1.6	4.7	2.4	2.7	5.7	3	8.5	5.8	0.6	3.1	2.1
Avg. Down Move	2.8	5.8	1.6	3.7	0.6	6.3	3.1	5.1	3.2	3.3	3.5	2.5
Greatest Up Move	0	3.9	6.2	3.2	4.8	8.7	3	8.5	8.2	0.7	4.2	2.3
Greatest Down Move	5	5.8	1.6	6.7	0.6	6.3	5.7	10.8	4.3	3.5	5.6	3.9

172

periods of time. If it is July, the trader may wish to analyze the situation for the period through December. This would allow him to utilize the August, October, and December contracts. He could, for instance, go long or short any combination of cattle versus any combination of hogs. It can be easily seen that there are many possible permutations of those three contracts. Thus the trader would come to some type of decision on the value of hogs in August, September, October, November, and December. He would go through the same exercise with the cattle. He would then compare those two values with the spread as seen in the futures market. If there are significant differences between his projections and the current spread values, then there is potential for profit. Develop your own forecasting equation to help you in determining value. Alternatively, the trader could use the seat of the pants approaches. A final technique would be to use technical analysis to determine future patterns in the outright positions and to combine them into a spread trade.

A further consideration for the cattle/hog spread trader is the seasonality of cattle and hogs. We have reproduced two more charts (Figures 13.3 and 13.4) that the reader should find useful in determining some cattle/hog spread ideas. Any time that the spread trader sees an increasing price in one commodity and a decreasing price in the other commodity, he should be thinking of putting on a spread during that time period. Another consideration is that both commodities may be increasing at the same time or decreasing at the same time but that one commodity increases or decreases more than the other. This can also lead to profit potential.

CRUSH SPREADS

The most complex spread is the crush spread. This is used extensively by soybean crushers as a hedge mechanism. It involves the purchase or sale of soybean contracts with the opposite transaction in the two products made from soybeans, soybean oil and soybean meal.

There are two separate spreads that can be achieved with these three commodities. One is the crush spread and the other is the reverse crush spread.

The first spread, also called "putting on the crush," is a duplication of soybean crusher transactions. The crush spread entails buying one contract of soybean futures and selling one contract each of soybean oil and soybean meal.

Soybean crushing or processing as a business requires a premium of the value of the meal and oil over the value of the soybeans. The soybean crusher receives profit largely depending on the margin between the products and the beans. This difference is called the *gross processing margin*. The soybean processor must buy soybeans, crush them into its components, meal and oil, and sell the meal and oil for a combined price higher than what he paid for his soybeans plus his other costs such as overhead and profit. Many soybean crushers hedge their crushing by putting on the crush spread. They are typically trying to lock in a profitable crush margin instead of leaving the profits to the vagaries of the marketplace.

The crush spread is particularly attractive during periods of large supply of the products and a strong demand for the soybeans. The soybean demand could potentially be from exports. Traders should watch the weekly and monthly crush figures as a clue to the actions of the soybean crushers. By watching these figures the spread trader may be able to tell whether the soybean crushers are reducing their crush due to a lack of profitability. The spreader should not be confused, however, by the normal period of shutdown around Labor Day and Christmas. Crushings take a sharp drop during those two periods as soybean processors shut their plants for their staff to take holidays and for routine maintenance to be done. Traders should also be examining the cash crush margins at all times, as they also give a clue to the current conditions in the marketplace.

There is also a seasonality to crush margins. They tend to be widest, that is, the products are worth the most compared to the beans, just at harvest time. This makes perfect sense when you consider that harvest time is the point of the greatest supply of the soybeans and at the same time may be the period of strong demand for meal and oil.

The most common speculative spread is the reverse crush spread. It is the opposite of what a soybean crusher would be doing in the marketplace. As was mentioned previously, sometimes the gross processing margin will deteriorate to a point where there is little or no profit in crushing soybeans. This typically comes about as an overproduction of the meal and oil in the fact of a relatively strong market in soybeans. It is difficult to ascertain exactly when soybean crushing becomes unprofitable. Depending on where they are and how much hedging they have done and what percentage of their capacity they are running at, the minimum crush margin necessary to provide a profit can vary from company to company and even over a wide area within a particular company.

When the gross processing margin becomes unprofitable, the soybean processor begins to think of reducing or stopping the processing of soybeans. Typically, the soybean crusher will continue to process soybeans for some time after moving into an unprofitable situation. This is not as crazy as it sounds at first. The loss on the processing of soybeans is usually less than the loss that the crusher will suffer if he had no revenue coming in. Even without processing any soybeans, the processor must continue to pay heat, light, financing charges on inventory, and so on. There may also be labor problems if the crusher is continually shutting down and reopening. It is often a more prudent plan to lose a small amount of money on the processing of beans rather than more money by shutting down. Also, the plant will sometimes lose less money if it processes a lot of soybeans than when it produces just a few. The higher the production is as a percentage of capacity, the more efficient the processing. Thus the per unit cost of processing is reduced.

Nonetheless, after a few months of losing money, soybean processors will begin to cut back production or shut down entirely. They will sometimes move from a two-shift schedule to a one-shift schedule or take an extra week of vacation near Labor Day or Christmas.

The eventual aim of cutting back production is to decrease the apparent surplus of soybean products on the marketplace. This obviously does not happen overnight. It can take several months for an apparent surplus to be worked down to a level which increases the gross processing margins. Thus the reverse crush spreader typically does not have to rush into positions.

The crush and reverse crush spreader should note that the crush margins usually trade within a wide range. Crush spreads placed at the high end of this range and reverse crushings put on at the low end can be a very profitable strategy. Over the long run, this strategy has been successful. It does, however, require nerves of steel and a large bankroll. It is not uncommon for a crush margin to go against the trader by 10, 20, or 30 cents. This is particularly true of the crush spread. The reverse crush spread, though theoretically of less risk, can also have positions move against it by tens of cents. It is obvious that the situation will eventually return to normal, but the spread trader must be well heeled in order to withstand the margin calls.

Another issue that the crush and reverse crush spreader must consider is the ratio of the various contracts to each other. The exchanges allow the placing of crush and reverse crush spreads in the ratio of one meal and one oil contract for every one soybean contract. Unfortunately, the number of bushels in one soybean contract does not yield the number of tons of soybean meal and number of pounds of soybean oil in one contract each. Nonetheless, spreaders should be aware that most brokerage houses will allow the crush and reverse crush spread for the margin necessary to carry just the soybeans. Commission rates are also occasionally reduced, though this is less common.

CASH INTERCOMMODITY SPREADS

One major factor that every intercommodity spreader must examine is the spread in the underlying cash commodities. For instance, should the trader be spreading wheat versus corn, she must be looking at what the cash spread is at the same time. A trader wishing to go long December wheat and short December corn at $1.50 premium the wheat would be well advised to reconsider the position if cash wheat is selling for 30¢ more than cash corn in November. It is well to remember that in the final analysis, the futures prices must be very close to the cash prices when the futures contracts expire. Also, typically, the futures prices will move more to reach the cash prices. This is mainly true just before the contract expires.

The examination of cash spreads in relation to futures spreads can give many ideas for the spread traders. It is infrequent that the cash spreads will be running close to the futures spreads except for those contracts that are nearest to expiring. There is no doubt, however, that the examination of the cash spreads as well as the futures spreads adds to the analytical task. Typically, this is not such a great problem as most spread traders spend a tremendous amount of time analyzing the underlying cash commodity anyway. Nonetheless, the added complexity may be enough to turn some traders from the use of the examination of cash commodity spreads.

TREASURY BOND VERSUS GINNIE MAE SPREADS

A popular intercommodity spread has risen in the last few years. The advent of interest rate futures in 1975 created new opportunities for spread traders. A particularly favorite spread is the intercommodity spread of Treasury Bonds versus GNMAs. GNMAs are government-backed mortgages that are commonly called Ginnie Maes.

Traders should note that people in the interest rate futures field call this particular spread an intermarket spread, although both Treasury Bonds and Ginnie Maes are traded on the same market, the Chicago Board of Trade. A true intermarket spread would be the spread between Chicago Board of Trade Treasury Bond futures versus the New York Futures Exchange Treasury Bond futures. In the interest rate futures field, the Treasury Bond versus Ginnie Mae spread is called an intermarket spread. In fact, it is referred to as *the* intermarket spread, as if no other intermarket spread existed.

The Treasury Bond contract calls for delivery of a thirty-year Treasury Bond while the Ginnie Mae contract calls for the delivery of a debt instrument of twelve-year duration. Thus a spread between the two commodities is largely affected by changes in the yield curve.

Although a discussion of the yield curve is beyond the scope of this book, let's hit a couple of the high points. A yield curve is simply a curve formed by points on a graph representing the length of the maturity versus the yield. A positive yield curve, as seen in Figure 13.5, has the yields increasing as maturities get more deferred. This is considered a normal yield curve. Figure 13.6 illustrates a flat yield curve, a yield curve in which all maturities are yielding approximately the same. A negative yield curve, seen in Figure 13.7, is the opposite of a positive yield curve. That is, short-term interest rates are yielding more than long-term interest rates. There are also variations of these, as seen in Figure 13.8, the humpback yield curve.

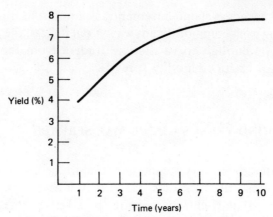

Figure 13.5   Positive yield curve.

As the yield curve changes, the spread changes. If the market goes from a positive yield curve to a negative yield curve the Treasury Bonds will gain on the Ginnie Maes. As the yield curve shifts, the shorter term instrument, the Ginnie Mae, will lose value to the longer term instrument, the Treasury Bond. Remember, when interest rates go up, the interest rate futures prices will go down. This explains why the bonds will gain on the Ginnies. When the yield curve goes from negative curve to a positive curve, the Ginnies will gain on the bonds for exactly the inverse of the reason given above.

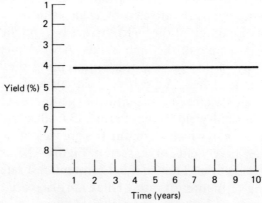

Figure 13.6   Flat yield curve.

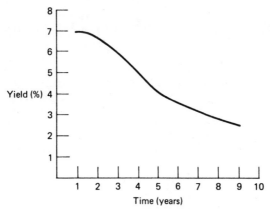

Figure 13.7   Negative yield curve.

Most of the time the trader will be trading a change in the yield curve that is not going from negative to positive or vice versa. The trader will be mainly looking for a change in the slope of a positive or negative yield curve. Thus he is looking for the slope to go either more or less positive or negative.

Let's examine several of the other major factors that are peculiar to the trading of just this particular spread. The first major factor is that periods of disintermediation reduce the demand for Ginnie Maes and increase the demand for Treasury Bonds. Disintermediation is when

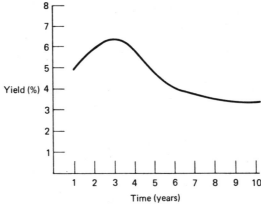

Figure 13.8   Humpback yield curve.

more money is taken out of savings and loans and thrift institutions than is deposited. Because savings and loans and thrift institutions are major purchasers of Ginnie Maes, their lack of funds to purchase them reduces the price of Ginnie Maes and hence reduces the price of Ginnie Maes relative to Treasury Bonds.

A second major factor to consider is housing starts. An increase in housing starts typically means an increase in the supply of Ginnie Maes. The more housing starts there are, the more Ginnie Maes need to be created to finance the housing starts. Thus on rising housing starts the trader would want to sell Ginnie Maes and buy Treasury Bonds and when housing starts are low the spread trader would prefer to buy Ginnies and sell bonds.

In a situation where the yield curve shifts up, the Ginnie Mae yields increase 1%, the price change in Treasury bonds will be greater than that for the Ginnie Maes. Because of the longer maturity, it requires more of a price movement to make the same percentage change. In other words, the bond price must move more to adjust to the new yield level.

Another factor affecting this spread is the season. It seems strange to consider that interest rates may have a seasonal factor, but because housing starts occur mainly in the summer, the supply of Ginnie Maes is increased during the summer while being decreased during the winter when fewer houses are built.

A heavy corporate bond calendar will often put pressure on the Treasury Bond futures more than the Ginnie Mae market. This is because corporate bonds typically are of long-term duration and thus compete more with the long-term Bonds rather than the intermediate-term Ginnie Maes. Furthermore, the corporate treasurers will hedge their purchases and sales of corporate bonds in the Treasury Bond market rather than the Ginnie Mae market.

Another consideration is the quarterly treasury refundings every February, May, August, and November. The Treasury sells large numbers of long-term Treasury Bonds at each of these quarterly refundings. Thus there is a temporary glut of Treasury Bonds relative to Ginnie Maes. Traders should be particularly alert for these as they can move the Treasury Bond/Ginnie Mae spread a significant amount each quarter. These may be used as trading opportunities in and of themselves or as opportunities to initiate or liquidate spreads.

A last note on nomenclature. A bull spread in this Treasury Bond/Ginnie Mae spread is considered to be long Treasury Bonds, short Ginnie Maes. The bear spread is long Ginnie Maes and short T-Bonds.

As was mentioned under intermarket spreads, it is often better to trade different months rather than the same months. Traders should be alert and use trading techniques to select the best months to be long and short in the various commodities.

SHORT SQUEEZES

Short squeezes can also warp relationships. The trader should be alert as to whether the short squeeze is a lack of nearby deliverable supplies, a factor that will be cleared up by the next delivery period, or whether it is a definite fundamental shortage that will last some time. It is wise that the trader be alert to short squeeze possibilities. The most important clues to a possible short squeeze are low deliverable stocks and large open interest. Both of these factors become more important the closer it is to first notice day, and they become even more important the closer it is to the last trading day. As mentioned above, the supply and demand for deliverable stocks are the final determinants of futures prices. In the final days of trading, a short squeeze can occur when there is a large open interest composed of longs who want to take delivery of a small deliverable stock. The short squeeze can push the price of one contract dramatically away from the other contracts.

It is important to note that trading spreads where one leg could be or is being short squeezed is a very high-stakes game. The trader should have a lot of backup capital and a good knowledge of cash markets.

FOURTEEN

The Trading Plan

We have now discussed several techniques of trading commodity spreads. The trading plan ties together all the techniques discussed. It focuses the trader's mind on the specific trade.

It is probably not exaggerating to say that the trading plan may be the most important part of any trade. The trading plan helps enforce the discipline necessary to execute a particular spread trade. What is the use of doing excellent research and discovering a trade possibility if the trader does not have the self-discipline to utilize the potential? There are many traders who do excellent research and have excellent techniques but do not have the self-discipline to trade their own ideas. When a position goes against them, they begin to act like inexperienced speculators. They begin to justify and rationalize why the price will begin to go up, and at the same time allow the price to continue to move against them. Conversely, as prices move in their favor, they are quick to take a profit, justifying their action by claiming, "You can't go broke taking a profit." In fact, such traders have just limited their profits.

The trading plan is devised before the trader has money on the line. This allows the trader to become more objective in analyzing and examining the various trade possibilities. Emotions are not yet being whipsawed by price movements. It is much easier to think rationally and logically before money has been committed to a trade than after the trade has been initiated and the trader is on the firing line.

The trading plan also allows the trader to analyze trades after they have been liquidated. This postmortem gives traders the opportunity to examine their techniques in a rational manner. Because the trading plan should contain most factors necessary for justifying a trade, traders are able to examine whether or not the problem factors were analyzed. Traders are able to see if some factors were underestimated or not considered or even overestimated. This feedback will aid traders in analyzing their trading strengths and weaknesses. They are given the opportunity to discover which of the factors they examined were important and which were not. Traders thus will be able to focus more clearly on the important factors in the future. The trading plan accomplishes many of the goals by providing a record of the thoughts of the analyst before the trade is initiated. It is this feature that provides an anchor for the analyst after he or she has entered a trade. Traders can ask themselves whether the trade and its influencing factors are unfolding as they had anticipated. If the factors are not unfolding as they had anticipated, are the unexpected changes in favor of or against the trade?

The trading plan will provide the distance necessary to make rational decisions after the trader has entered the trade. It can contribute to calmness and peace of mind. It can help prevent sleepless nights when a trader is worrying about what the next move should be in a particular trade.

A trading plan, although it takes a significant amount of time to fill out, actually saves a lot of time. Often, traders without trading plans spend a large portion of their trading time merely watching every tick as the commodity is trading. They appear to think that if they were not watching the market, it would go against them. Because the trading plan gives the trader's rationale for entering and exiting a trade as well as the actual entry and exit points, the trader no longer has to watch each tick. Orders are placed before the market opens and if they get filled, they get filled. If orders are not filled, the trader stays in the position and examines the entry and exit points again at the end of the day. Because the trader's decisions are made in a cool state of mind, each tick need not be examined. It appears to be difficult for a trader to stay in a position while the price is moving sharply toward the predetermined stop loss point. There is apparently a natural impulse to exit the trade before the stop is hit. Once again, however, the exit point should be at a logical point that will support the position. Impulsive behavior may eliminate a profitable trade. By saving the spread trader from having to watch each tick, the trader releases time which can be used more profitably by analyzing new positions and developing new trading tools.

All of these comments on the use of a trading plan as an aide to self-discipline are useless if the trader does not follow the plan. There is little doubt that a written trading plan provides a greater incentive for self-discipline than a mental plan does. A mental plan is more likely to be the trader's wishful thinking rather than a well-thought-out, logical plan. A written plan will tend to be more complete and takes into account all factors that the trader must consider before entering a position. The written plan, which would most likely consist of spaces to be filled out on a form, is more convenient than trying to remember all possible factors. The mental plan has a severe problem in that it relies on the trader's memory. The trader's memory can be faulty and affected by emotion. Let's face it: people remember mainly what they wish to remember. A written plan also provides the trader with the opportunity to conduct a postmortem on the trade. It is for all these reasons that the trader should be using only a written plan.

A trading plan should contain sections for each major element of the trade. Each trade that the spreader considers should be analyzed from four points of view. The spread trader should look at the technical, seasonal, historical, and fundamental aspects of the market before initiating a trade. The trader may decide to ignore one or more of these factors in making the decision, but the trader should be conditioned to taking at least a glance at each of the different facets. Suppose that a trader wanted to put on a corn spread which was 95% of full carry, only because of the closeness to full carry. He might say that there is no need to examine technical or seasonal factors. It may be, however, that even a brief review of these factors will show that the spread has only a small chance of working. Perhaps the seasonal tendency is to move to 100% of full carry.

One can easily find circumstances where the trader would be wasting time by examining all four facets of analysis. Most traders, however, will see better results if they form the habit of examining the four aspects on all trades. There may be the odd circumstance of wasting time, but this will be more than compensated by increased profitability.

In addition to the sections devoted to the four trading factors mentioned above, there must also be a section devoted to general information such as the name of the commodity and the date. A second additional section would be a summary based on the four factors examined. A last section which should be included is the action section. This section details the position and the entry and exit points. It may be considered the culmination of the whole trading plan.

Let us examine more closely a specific trading plan. The plan that we will examine is a plan that the author uses as an outline of approaching a particular trade. The trader who feels it does not meet her needs should add sections or delete sections as she sees fit. The author encourages the readers to experiment with this form and to develop better ones.

The first area on the trading plan is the general area. The date that goes into the date section should be the date that the trading plan is filled out, thus providing a record of when the analysis was done. The commodity section is where the trader puts down the commodity or commodities that are being traded. In the contracts section, the trader lists the contract months to be traded. Thus a July/January soybean

---

The following must be filled out before initiating any trade.

General

Date _____ Commodity(s) _____ Contract(s) _____

Margin _____ each.   Commission _____ each.

Technical

Chart trend: long term _____ intermediate _____ short _____

Chart support: _____

Chart resistance: _____

Formations: _____

_____

Commitments of traders: _____

Volume and open interest considerations: _____

_____

Contract high _____ low _____

Optimized moving average combination: _____

Bullish consensus _____ last week _____

Technical comments _____

_____

_____

Figure 14.1   The trading plan.

Seasonal

Monthly period from _____ to _____ percent reliable _____

Average move _____ average up _____ average down _____

Greatest up _____ greatest down _____

Weekly period from _____ to _____ percent reliable _____

Average move _____ average up _____ average down_____

Greatest up _____ greatest down _____

Seasonal comments _____

_____

_____

_____

Historical
1. What year(s) was/were similar to this year?
2. What indicators and factors were similar?
3. What indicators and factors were different?
4. What effect will the differences have?
5. What happened to the price in the similar year(s)?
6. What is projected to happen this year?

Fundamental
1. What is the supply situation?
2. What is the demand situation?
3. What is the balance between them?
4. What is projected to happen this year?

Conclusion and Scenario(s)
1. Why put on the trade?
2. What indicators are favorable and what indicators are not?
3. What could happen to cause the position to fail?
4. Describe scenario(s) of what might happen.

Action

Position: long _____ short _____

Initiate position at _____

Initial stop loss: _____

Use a trailing stop? yes _____ no _____

    if yes, how many points _____ from _____ (previous close? high?)

Figure 14.1 (*continued*)

spread will have soybeans listed in the commodity section and July/ January in the contract section. It should be noted that the trading plan can be used for outright positions as well and that is why a single contract should be placed in that space. The margin section is where the trader enters the margin required by the broker. This can be useful when the trader wants to know the amount of capital left for investing. The commissions section also contains information that the trader may find useful.

The next area on the chart is the technical area. The chart trend allows the trader to put down whether the long-term, intermediate, or short-term trends are up, neutral, or down. This would be found by some type of mechanical trading system or, more usually, through chart analysis.

The chart support sections allows the trader to list the nearest chart support points. The blank space is left purposely long so that the trader can place quite a few chart support points if necessary. The same comments apply to the chart resistance section except that the technical short trader will be examining resistance points rather than support points. The formations section is devoted to listing various chart formations, such as pennants, flags, and downtrend lines.

The commitment of traders section is for the trader to list the positions of other market participants as outlined in the Commitments of Traders Report issued by the Commodity Futures Trading Commission. This is of particular importance for outright positions but also has much relevance when trading spreads. For instance, by examining the report, the trader may find that large speculators are long the new crop and short the old crop wheat. Because large speculators are usually considered to be smart money, the trader may wish to look more closely at the bear spreads in wheat after examining the Commitment of Traders Report.

Volume and open interest considerations are placed in the next section. The contract highs and lows go in the succeeding sections. The trader may find these useful for delineating support and resistance points as well as providing some type of risk or reward points. The following section, optimized moving average combination, can be adapted by the trader to provide an informational section for what is the best trend-following or countertrend system that the trader wishes to use. In our example, a moving average is used. Once again, the reader is encouraged to discover trading systems that work well.

The bullish consensus for the current and preceding weeks are listed in the next two sections. This is useful for the contrarian, who may utilize that information for the entering and exiting of spread positions.

After filling out all of these sections, the technician will then fill out the summary and conclusion for the technical area. This summary and conclusion is placed in the technical comments section. It should have some type of conclusion as well as possible entering and exit points.

The third area on the trading plan is the seasonal area. Here monthly and weekly seasonality is examined and placed on the trading plan. The source for seasonal patterns in spreads can be from the trader's own work, books, or computer services. Depending on the format of the seasonality, the trading plan will follow the format outlined in the example or have to be adopted to the different format. The format used in the example was the format used in *Profits Through Seasonal Trading* (by Jack Grushcow and Courtney Smith, Ronald Press, 1980). No matter what format the trader decides to use, it should include a summary and conclusion section. This section, entitled seasonal comments on the sample trading plan, should provide a conclusion and recommendation for the best time to enter and exit the trade.

The next section, the historical section, does not use a fill-in-the-blanks approach as did the previous section. Here the trader must answer the questions on a separate sheet of paper. The questions are not considered a definitive list but more a tool to jog the memory and force the trader to consider the major points. A more complete list of questions would almost duplicate the chapter on historical comparison analysis in this book.

Much the same type of situation exists in the following area, called the fundamental area. Here, even more, the questions are so vague as to be almost meaningless. They exist merely as a spark to the trader. The questions cannot be broken down into more detail because of the wide variety of possible commodities that may be discussed. For example, a question about export projections may be sensible for soybeans but is ridiculous for GNMAs. Thus the fundamental area relies on the depth of thought and self-discipline of the trader more than the other areas do.

The conclusion and scenario area concisely wraps up the four major factors into a summary form. It should refer to the sections preceding it. It becomes almost a balance sheet where the trader is totaling up the factors that he believes are in favor of the trade and those considered unfavorable to the trade. A second function of this area is to list what could possibly go wrong and why. Analyzing potential hazards can often dissuade the trader from putting on a trade. The last point in the conclusion and scenario section is the narration of one or more possible scenarios to state how the trader thinks the various factors will develop. If the trader expects certain fundamental or technical events, these should be detailed along with some ideas of a time frame.

The scenario should describe milestones which the trader can check to confirm that the trade is still valid and has the prospect for making money. Alternatively, the milestones may show that the trade is no longer viable and will not provide a profit.

The action area is the real conclusion of the trading plan. It is here that the actual desired position is detailed. The position section shows which contract or contracts the trader wishes to be long or short. The following section gives the trader room to describe the point at which the trade should be initiated. This can be a specific price or can be a technical parameter such as breaking the trend line or whatever the trader feels is a good entry technique. For money management reasons, the trader should be placing an initial stop loss in the section that follows. From that point on the trader can answer the questions that follow. Is there going to be a trailing stop or is the trader going to use some other technical or fundamental rationale for exiting the trade? Is there an objective to the trade and will the trader exit the position should the trade reach his objective? If the trader is using a trailing stop, she uses the section that talks about how far the stop is placed from the previous close, high, or low. Some people prefer to have their trailing stops follow on a close-only basis. Others prefer to use the extremes of a particular price, whether this is a recent high or a recent low. For simplification purposes, the form says high but this should be considered by the reader to imply low as well.

A second factor in the successful use of a trading plan is monitoring the trade's progress. For this, a weekly sheet should recap what has happened in the preceding week and provide the trader the opportunity to reexamine and reestablish the discipline needed for successful trading. The weekly sheet is basically a summary of the trading plan. Notice in Figure 14.2 that the sections follow a similar plan.

General

Date _____ Commodity(s) _____ Contract(s) _____
Number of positions _____ Margin _____ each. Commission _____ each.
Government reports this week _____

Action

Position: long _____ short _____
Initiate(d) position at _____
Use a trailing stop? yes _____ no _____
    if yes, how many points _____ from _____ (previous close? high?)
    if no, then where? _____

Technical

Price _____ last week _____
Chart trend: long term _____ intermediate _____ short _____
Chart support: _____
Chart resistance: _____
Formations: _____
Commitments of Traders: _____ Moving average _____ last week _____
Volume: this week _____ % change _____
        last week _____ % change _____ prior week _____
Open interest: this week _____ % change _____
        last week _____ % change _____ prior week _____
Contract high _____ low _____ last week's high _____ low _____
Bullish consensus _____ last week _____
Technical comments _____
_____

Seasonal

From _____ to _____ percent reliable _____
Average move _____ average up _____ average down _____
Greatest up _____ greatest down _____
Seasonal comments _____
_____

Historical/Fundamental

1. Is this year following previous similar year(s)?
2. Comment.
3. Any short term fundamental factors worth commenting on?
4. Is the fundamental situation developing as predicted?
5. Comment.
6. Any new factors not accounted for in the Trading Plan?
7. Conclusion?

Figure 14.2 The weekly sheet.

191

One significant difference is that the action section is placed near the beginning of the sheet rather than at the end. This is done because at this point the action has occurred and is the most significant part of the trading plan. During the trading plan phase, the trader was more concerned with justifying and examining all the possibilities rather than the actual exit and entry points. Once the trader has entered the position, however, the actual entry and exit positions become the paramount consideration.

Also note that the historical/fundamental sections have been combined into one area. Because the historical and fundamental analyses have already been completed, these two areas are devoted to commenting on current conditions. The point of the questions on the weekly sheet is mainly to examine the milestones that have been delineated on the trading plan. The major concern is whether or not the milestones are being reached as expected.

The importance of the trading plan and the weekly sheet cannot be overemphasized. Filling out the sheets helps to develop and maintain the discipline needed to trade commodities. There are those who consider the trading plan to be the most important part of any commodity trade. They believe that the trader can use almost any technique and make money as long as good money management is practiced and a trading plan is rigidly followed.

FIFTEEN

Trading Techniques

The mechanics of spread trading are relatively simple. The exchanges will accept fewer types of order for spreads than for outright positions.

The proper use of spread orders can be the difference between a profitable trade and an unprofitable trade. Because spreads require the simultaneous purchase and sale of two contracts, entry and exit are necessarily more difficult.

MARKET, LIMIT, AND TIME ORDERS

There are three types of spread order, each with a specific use. There are times when the trader will use one type of order and not another type. The trader, however, should check to see which of the orders described below are acceptable at which exchanges. Some exchanges take orders that other exchanges won't accept.

A *market order* is perhaps the most common type of order. The trader tells the broker how many spreads he wishes to buy or sell but does not specify the price at which he wishes to initiate the spreads. The order means to do the trade as quickly as possible at the best possible price.

The main purpose of a market order is speed, not the best possible price. The floor broker will attempt to get a good price but will spend only about ten seconds trying to find it. His goal is to make the trade quickly.

Market orders work well in a large liquid market. The floor broker can easily find other brokers willing to take the other side of the trade. The spread between the bid and ask prices is often the minimum tick for that commodity. Thus in June a popular spread like the July/November soybean spread can be filled at the market at the prevailing prices.

On the other hand, an illiquid market, having low volume or interest, can be treacherous to the trader using a market order. When the floor broker receives the order to execute an illiquid spread at the market, he may have a hard time finding another party to trade with.

Suppose it is June and a trader wants to initiate a long March/short May orange juice spread at about 100 points premium the May. The March/May orange juice spread will be illiquid in June. Even though March orange juice and May orange juice may settle 100 points apart for a month, the trader will have a difficult time obtaining that price.

The floor broker, after receiving the order, will have to find someone to take the other side of the transaction. As there are few trades in March orange juice and May orange juice and even fewer in the March/May orange juice spread, he will have to discount the spread more and more to induce someone to take the other side. The broker may have to offer more than 50 points to find a trading partner.

The trader, looking to obtain the spread at 100 points premium the May, now finds himself the unproud owner at 50 points premium the May. And yet, at the end of the day, the March and May contracts may continue to close 100 points apart.

A *limit order* can prevent the unfortunate experience of the orange juice spreader. A limit order specifies the price that the floor broker can accept for the trade. The trader instructs the broker to execute the trade at that price or better.

The orange juice spreader could have entered his order to buy March and sell May orange juice at 100 points premium May. The broker is being instructed to buy the March and sell May but only if he can sell the May at least 100 points higher than the March. The broker could not put the trade on by selling May 50 points or 60 points or, for that matter, 99 points above the March. The broker is allowed to obtain a better price than specified.

The drawback to the limit order is that no one may wish to take the other side of the spreader's offered trade. The orange juice spreader may offer 100 points premium May and nobody wants it. The orange juice spreader may never be able to put his spread on.

It is also possible for the trader to see the price move through his "limit price" on the tape or quote machine and yet not be guaranteed to be in the trade. It's possible that the trade took place on the opposite side of the pit and the floor broker didn't hear it or was unable to get there in time.

Further, it must be remembered that spread quotes frequently differ from the difference between the two outrights. That difference is a rough guide but may not represent the actual spread quotes. It is quite possible that one of the two contracts has not traded for some time and the other contract's price has moved away from the first one.

A *time order* specifies the time of day that the trader wishes her order to be filled. It may be at a particular time of day or, more commonly, on the open or close.

Thus the spread trader could conceivably put in an order like "buy June sell December silver at 11:15 a.m. central time." This would become a market order at 11:15.

Most time orders are orders to initiate or exit trades at the market on the open or close. A typical order might be to "buy August sell December live cattle, market on close."

INTERMARKET SPREAD ORDERS

Intermarket spread orders are the hardest to execute. The floor broker must buy a contract of one commodity at his market then quickly contact his counterpart in another market's pits.

The built-in delay makes it difficult for the broker to execute limit orders. Some brokers will accept intermarket spreads only on a "not held" basis. This means that they will try their best but will not be held responsible for poor executions. They do this to protect themselves from buying one market's contract, having the other market's price fall away from them, and being stuck holding the first contract because of an inability to get the required price on the other contract. Some brokers will accept intermarket limit spread orders on a "take your time" (TYT) basis. This gives the floor broker more time to use his discretion in executing the order.

There is no delay in getting an intermarket spread market order filled. The broker merely executes this spread as two separate market orders.

STOP ORDERS

A stop order is an order that becomes a market order as soon as a given price level is reached. Thus the order "buy July sell August pork bellies at 50 points premium July stop" becomes a market order if the July/August belly spread trades at 50 points or higher, premium July.

It should be noted, however, that few exchanges accept spread stop orders. The Chicago Board of Trade accepted them in the past but no longer does. (They were too much trouble for the floor brokers.) The Chicago Mercantile Exchange accepts them but only at the discretion of the floor broker.

For all practical purposes, traders should assume that they will not be able to use spread stop orders. Traders should check with their brokers to find out the latest policies.

Although spread stop orders may not exist, many spread advisors and traders act as if they did. Newsletters, advisors, and brokers often tell their clients to put on a spread with a stop at such-and-such a level. Some will even use the term "close only stop."

The terms "stop" and "close only stop" are not strictly correct but serve a useful purpose. These "stops" should be considered *mental stops*. The trader can enter market or limit orders when the spread appears to be trading at or near the exit point. This obviously requires more savvy on the part of the trader and her broker.

"Close only stops" are more complicated. The trade should look at the settlement or closing prices of the two legs of the spread. If the difference is not beyond the exit point, the trader does nothing. If it is past the "stop," he calls his broker just after the opening the following morning and asks for a quote on the spread. If the quote from the floor is also beyond the "stop," the trader should put in a market order or a limit order at the quoted price to offset his spread. If the floor quote is not beyond the "stop," the trader goes through the same cycle following the close that day.

ENTERING THE ORDER

The trader should obtain from her broker the latest spread quotes from the floor before entering any trades. This gives the trader the best indication of the price of the spread.

Alternatively, the trader should check the spread differences based on the settlement prices. Other than quotes direct from the floor, the settlement prices give the best indication of spread price levels.

Traders should use limit orders whenever possible. The spread trader is often looking for rather small changes in price differences. A market order may nullify whatever price advantage the spreader had.

Market orders should be used only when speed of execution is the paramount concern. This might be a concern if news causes dramatic moves in the market, and the trader wants to quickly enter or exit a position.

LEGGING IN OR OUT

Legging in is the process of putting on a spread by buying or selling one leg of the spread followed, some time in the future, by the selling or buying of the second leg. Legging out is the same process to exit a trade. Legging in or out turns an outright position into a spread or vice versa. It is usually done for the wrong reasons. The technique is only useful when the trader wants to convert an outright position into a spread or a spread into an outright.

The trader holding an outright position may decide that, for whatever reason, his outright position will no longer be a wise investment. Simultaneously, he discovers a good spread prospect that has, as one of its legs, the outright position the trader wishes to eliminate. The trader legs into the other side of the spread. Eventually, and most probably, the spread is liquidated as a spread.

The purpose of this exercise is to save a small amount of money on commissions. The trader does not liquidate his outright position, pay full commission for it, and then initiate the spread. Legging into the spread saves the trader half of a round turn commission.

Changing the outright position into a spread must be considered coincidental. That is, the two positions must have been considered as two separate trades that happened to coincide in time.

This will typically happen only when a major government report is to be released. A speculator, long August cattle, deems the situation too risky to carry her long position into the July 1 Cattle on Feed Report. She does believe that the report will be bullish but does not want to take on the additional risk going into the report. Rather than liquidating her long August position, she shorts December cattle. The speculator has reduced the risk substantially by shorting the December cattle. She has also substantially reduced the reward. The speculator has thus replaced a high-stake bet on the outcome of the report with a low-stake bet.

It should be noted that the trader may be right in the bullishness of the report and still lose money. The report might show fewer cattle on feed to be marketed in December than in August. This may force all contracts higher but may also force the December cattle to be stronger than the August cattle.

This demonstrates the need to consider the outright and the spread to be two different trades, each initiated and liquidated for its own reasons. It is too easy for the trader to use a simplistic approach when substituting spreads for outrights. They must be considered separate trades. The legging into the spread should be considered only as a minor commission saver.

Legging Mistakes

Most legging in and out is done for the wrong reasons. The most common mistake is to leg into a spread from an unprofitable outright position.

Suppose a trader is short December copper and is losing $2,000. The trader may not want to confront the fact that the loss in equity is a failure. He believes that by hanging onto the trade he has a chance to make back the loss. No one can disagree that the speculator has a chance to turn the trade into a winner, but at that moment, it is a failure.

Traders psychologically will often think that a realized loss of $2,000 is worse than an unrealized loss of $2,000. By realizing the loss, the trader feels forced to admit failure.

Faced with the potential for psychological trauma and the necessity of putting up more margin, the trader decides to stall for time by shorting March copper. The trader has drastically reduced his chance of losing any more money and has reduced his margin needs. Temporarily, he has forstalled the need to admit failure and has no need to put up more margin.

Nothing has been accomplished, however, except increased commission costs. By totally eliminating the losing outright he would have no margin requirements and would be psychologically free to look for new profit potentials. The chances of recouping his losses on the outright by profiting from the new spread position must be considered somewhere between slim and none. There is no point in locking in a loss by spreading.

Bad Spread into Good Outright

Much the same mistake, though less severe, is seen while legging out of spreads. Traders will seek to convert an unprofitable spread into a profitable outright.

Assume that a speculator is short December, long March copper and is currently losing $500. The speculator, seeing a downtrend developing in copper, decides to liquidate the long March copper and go just short December copper in an effort to regain the lost $500.

This is not a bad tactic if the speculator coincidentally decides that short December copper is a good trade and that short December/long March copper is a bad trade. However, these types of coincidences are rare. The speculator must have the discipline to mentally separate the spread and the outright positions. He must fight the fear of losing, a fear that might motivate him to compound his losses by legging out of a bad spread into a bad outright.

THE MULTIUNIT TACTIC

The multiunit tactic involves initiating spread positions in units of two or more. The same concepts would apply, with little modification, to positions of two or twenty. For simplicity, let us use two units as the example.

Positions should always be initiated in units of two or more. This will require more margin but will provide more trading flexibility and profit potential. If the position goes against the trader immediately after it is initiated, the trader should liquidate the position at her predetermined exit point. The trader has doubled her losses, but, using sound money management, this should not be fatal, or even hurt very much.

An alternative tactic would be to stagger the stop loss points. Exit one spread very close to the entry point and exit the second one farther from the exit point. The two exit points could be broken support levels or money management stops or whatever method the trader wishes to use. The staggered stop tactic allows the trader more flexibility in his stop loss exiting.

Suppose, though, that the trade becomes profitable. The trader has several tactics he can then use.

He can liquidate one spread as soon as it is profitable enough to ensure that the whole trade, including commissions, will break even. A spreader is short 10 July/long 10 December oats at 4 cents premium December. His commission cost is $75 per spread for a total of $150.

The spreader could liquidate one of the two spreads when it reaches 7¢ premium December, a $150 profit. The remaining spread's risk protection point or "stop" would be raised to 4¢ premium December. The effect of these two actions would be to ensure that the trade, as a whole, would break even. The $150 profit on the first spread would pay for both spread's commissions and the upping of the second spread's exit point to its entry point ensures it will not lose money. The remaining spread would then be carried as long as the price moved favorably or until the spreader's objective had been reached.

A second way to use the multiunit method is to liquidate the first unit when it has achieved the break-even point and has gained a predetermined profit, say 10–100% of margin invested.

The predetermined profit level can be set to any point the trader chooses. One possibility is to make it a set multiple of the risk level. If the spreader risked 3 cents total on his oat spreads, the first spread could be liquidated at, say, two times the risk, or 6¢. Once again, the second spread would be allowed to carry to more profitable levels and liquidated by whatever method the spreader deems appropriate.

The final multiunit tactic to be used when the spread is profitable is to hold one and trade one. In other words, one spread is held until a change in trend is detected and the other spread is initiated and liquidated on a shorter term technical point of view.

50 pts = $562

Figure 15.1   October/March sugar spread.

Figure 15.1 shows the price of the October 81/March 82 sugar spread. Suppose a brilliant trader decided to sell 2 October sugar and buy 2 March sugar at 450 points premium the October contract in November. Let us further suppose that he wants to hold one spread for a big move and trade the second one for 100 point profits. The speculator, being a technician, decides to sell another spread every time the price comes close to the downtrend line.

This tactic would have been very profitable as the spreader was able to collect 100 point profits several times. Finally, judging by Figure 15.1, he would have taken himself out of the market in the latter part of March as the spread price broke through the downtrend.

This example shows the potential in the hold and trade variation of the multiunit tactic.

SIXTEEN

Sources of Information

The following is a list of sources of information that will be of interest to spread traders. I have also prepared a packet of information on spreads that the reader may obtain by simply writing to Courtney Smith, 1614-675 West Hastings, Vancouver, B.C., V6R 4W3, Canada. Some brokerage houses also have information and even newsletters aimed at spread traders.

BOOKS

Commodity Spreads, by Ed Dobson, Traders Press, 1981, Box 10344, Greenville, SC 29603. This is the best book for the commodity spread trader. The book is composed of charts of spread price action going back to 1971. It is indispensable for using historical comparison analysis. It is also very useful for examining seasonal tendencies and obtaining prices for regression and correlation analysis. Highly recommended.

Odds-On Grain Spreading, by Wayne Esserman, Ewe Publishing, 1979, Box 201, Delphi, IN 46923. This is an examination of the monthly seasonality of intramarket wheat, corn, and soybean spreads. The method used to determine the seasonality is the examination of historical price patterns rather than the ratio to moving average method. Recommended for the grain spreader.

Viewpoints of a Commodity Trader, by Roy Longstreet, Traders Press, 1967, Box 10344, Greenville, SC 29603. Although not written with the spreader in mind, this book has much that is useful. The psychological aspect of trading is the main subject. Recommended for all traders.

The Commodity Futures Game, by Richard Teweles, Charles Harlow, and Herbert Stone, McGraw-Hill Book Company, 1974, New York. This is the best overview of the commodity futures market. A chapter is devoted to spreads but the emphasis of the book is on presenting information on virtually every aspect of commodity trading. The breadth of coverage is excellent and the depth is above average. The best book on commodities for the novice stuck on a desert island.

Commodity Trading Systems and Methods, by Perry Kaufman, John Wiley & Sons, New York, 1978. Perry Kaufman has done a remarkable job assembling and explaining just about every technical trading system or method you have ever heard of. The depth of knowledge is amazing and the rigorousness of thought should be emulated by every commodity writer. This book tells you almost everything you wanted to know about technical trading but were too poor to afford. There is nothing about spreads in this book but many of the techniques could be adapted to spread trading. Should be on the bookshelf of every commodity trader.

PERIODICALS

Spread Scope, Box 5841, Mission Hills, CA 91345. No spread trader can be without a subscription to *Spread Scope*. It is a weekly chart service totally devoted to spread price charts. It is timely and complete. One very useful feature is the table of carrying charges at the back of each issue. Highly recommended. The same company also publishes an advisory letter which analyzes spreads from a technical perspective.

Commodity Spread Trader, Hadady Publications, 61 South Lake Avenue, Suite 309, Pasadena, CA 91101. This is a biweekly publication that issues specific spread suggestions. A telephone recorder message comes with the service. They have had a good track record but need more space devoted to justifying the suggested spreads.

Commodities Magazine, 219 Parkade, Cedar Falls, IA 50613. An occasional article on spreads shows up here. There is also much that is generally useful for the commodity trader. Recommended.

APPENDIX

Critical Values of *t*

Level of Significance for One-Tailed Test

.10	.05	.025	.01	.005	.0005

Level of Significance for Two-Tailed Test

df	.20	.10	.05	.02	.01	.001
1	3.078	6.314	12.706	31.821	63.657	636.619
2	1.886	2.920	4.303	6.965	9.925	31.598
3	1.638	2.353	3.182	4.541	5.841	12.941
4	1.533	2.132	2.776	3.747	4.604	8.610
5	1.476	2.015	2.571	3.365	4.032	6.859
6	1.440	1.943	2.447	3.143	3.707	5.959
7	1.415	1.895	2.365	2.998	3.499	5.405
8	1.397	1.860	2.306	2.896	3.555	5.041
9	1.383	1.833	2.262	2.821	3.250	4.781
10	1.372	1.812	2.228	2.764	3.169	4.587
11	1.363	1.796	2.201	2.718	3.106	4.437
12	1.356	1.782	2.179	2.681	3.055	4.318
13	1.350	1.771	2.160	2.650	3.012	4.221
14	1.345	1.761	2.145	2.624	2.977	4.140
15	1.341	1.753	2.131	2.602	2.947	4.073

Level of Significance for Two-Tailed Test

df	.20	.10	.05	.02	.01	.001
16	1.337	1.746	2.120	2.583	2.921	4.015
17	1.333	1.740	2.110	2.567	2.898	3.965
18	1.330	1.734	2.101	2.552	2.878	3.922
19	1.328	1.729	2.093	2.539	2.861	3.883
20	1.325	1.725	2.086	2.528	2.845	3.850
21	1.323	1.721	2.080	2.518	2.831	3.819
22	1.321	1.717	2.074	2.508	2.819	3.792
23	1.319	1.714	2.069	2.500	2.807	3.767
24	1.318	1.711	2.064	2.492	2.797	3.745
25	1.316	1.708	2.060	2.485	2.787	3.725
26	1.315	1.706	2.056	2.479	2.779	3.707
27	1.314	1.703	2.052	2.473	2.771	3.690
28	1.313	1.701	2.048	2.467	2.763	3.674
29	1.311	1.699	2.045	2.462	2.756	3.659
30	1.310	1.697	2.042	2.457	2.750	3.646
40	1.303	1.684	2.021	2.423	2.704	3.551
60	1.296	1.671	2.000	2.390	2.660	3.460
120	1.289	1.658	1.980	2.358	2.617	3.373
∞	1.282	1.645	1.960	2.326	2.576	3.291

This table is abridged from Table III of Fisher and Yates: *Statistical Tables for Biological, Argicultural, and Medical Research*, published by Oliver and Boyd Ltd., Edinburgh, by permission of the authors and publishers.

Index

209